ED W

27

ED WOOD

Scott Alexander
and Larry Karaszewski

faber and faber
LONDON BOSTON

First published in Great Britain in 1995
by Faber and Faber Limited
3 Queen Square London WC1N 3AU

Photoset by Parker Typesetting Service, Leicester
Printed in England by Clays Ltd, St Ives plc

A CIP record for this book
is available from the British Library

ISBN 0-571-17568-6

This book could not have been done
without the generous assistance of
Jennifer Casey, Kathy Nolda,
Katy James, Michelle Sewell
and, especially, Hunter Heller.

2 4 6 8 10 9 7 5 3 1

Introduction
by Scott Alexander and Larry Karaszewski

Why write a movie about Ed Wood?

Orson Welles never got a biopic. Alfred Hitchcock never got a biopic. So why go to the trouble of glorifying a guy who's famous simply because he's no good? Well, this requires a bit of explaining . . .

In the 1950s, Edward D. Wood, Jr. began making movies. Working in a world of grade-Z programmers intended for drive-ins and grindhouses, Ed didn't actually produce useable exploitation. His films were less concerned with entertainment value than with getting his obsessions and strange passions expressed on the screen. Angora, dead bodies, space monsters, old cowboy actors, pleas for universal tolerance, stock footage . . . Ed felt compelled to make cloth out of these burning issues. And if the result was bewilderment and boredom . . . so be it.

Unfortunately, Ed's six features were more than flops; some weren't even released. Potential backers became nonexistent. Disheartened, he slid into pornography and heavy drinking. The '60s and '70s were rough on him, and when Ed Wood died in 1978, he was penniless and forgotten.

However, whimsical Fate had special plans waiting for him. Thus, a mere two years later, Harry and Michael Medved wrote a book, *The Golden Turkey Awards*, in which Ed was proclaimed The Worst Director Of All Time. Suddenly, he became a brand name overnight. Fan clubs and bad movie festivals sprang up everywhere. Ed Wood was now a superstar, but with a heavy price to pay: people were laughing *at* him, ridiculing his incompetence, crossdressing, and pathetic lifestyle.

At the time, the two of us were college room-mates, and like others, astonished at the Wood phenomenon. One of us (Scott) even proposed an Ed Wood documentary, 'The Man In The Angora Sweater', for a film class. The teachers weren't impressed. As our screenwriting career began, we often joked about an Ed Wood biopic, collecting every article and scrap of information about him

v

we could find. But until 1992, it didn't seem relevant enough to pursue.

That year, we had a career crisis. After writing the enormously profitable *Problem Child* films, we had become trapped in a kiddie movie ghetto. Nobody would hire us to write anything else. This was quite frustrating, since our original script had actually been an adult black comedy. But we had been fired, and the project had been systematically 'dumbed down'. Although the final result made buckets of money, it was universally reviled – and our reputations were quite shaky. It's hard to garner respect when you have critics saying the script 'wasn't written, it was fingerpainted', or 'it seems to have been written by a demented proctologist'.

After this nonstop assault, we knew what it was like to be mercilessly ridiculed. People didn't care that it takes just as much hard work to make a bad movie as a good one – maybe more – and we started identifying with Ed Wood.

So with no paycheck on the horizon, and wishing to do something to reinvigorate our lives and our careers, we started preparing a treatment for an Ed Wood biopic. Before the *Problem Child* experience, we probably would have written a campy, mean-spirited Ed Wood film – the obvious approach. But now, after our critical lambasting, we looked at Ed in a different light. Sympathetically.

We conceived *Ed Wood* as a rebuttal to the usual film biography: The Great Man Story. We saw Ed as an Anti-Great Man, a loser who could never get things right. In most people's eyes, he is a nanosecond blip in world history – unworthy of study. Yet we saw a subversive purity, a screwball who wouldn't compromise his vision, even though he was ferociously wrong. An Anti-Great Man presents enormous drama, because he is constantly irritating everybody. The conflict is inherent. The story suddenly presented fascinating ironic challenges: our job was to get the audience rooting for Ed to make his movies badly – because that's why he was loved and remembered.

The process was exhilarating. We were writing from the heart, creating something strange and unusual. We wanted to create a cast of fruitcakes, drug addicts and outcasts, dreamers on the absolute fringe, then make them lovable. At this point, we also brought in our old friend Michael Lehmann, cajoling him into getting involved as director. Michael was just coming off the *Hudson Hawk* debacle, and we thought, 'Isn't this hilarious – the director of *Hudson Hawk* and the writers of *Problem Child* making a movie about the worst film-maker of all time? How apropos!'

But it made sense. We were in similar funks, and it seemed like a way to get back to our creative roots, by doing something small and independent. Knowing we would need help to get this crazy movie made, Michael suggested taking the treatment to Denise DiNovi, who had produced his film *Heathers*. At the time, she was partnered with Tim Burton, and his involvement as producer would surely help get financing. So Tim read the treatment – and flipped. Not only did he want to produce it, he wanted to direct it! After many discussions, he and Michael made a deal: they would swap roles. Tim could be director, contingent upon *Ed Wood* being his next film.

We had a brief meeting with Mr Burton. He loved our odd tone, a balance of funny and sad. His only note was quite simple: be careful with the crossdressing. Finally, terribly excited and eager, he turned to us and said, 'When can I see a script?'

We hadn't been hired, but we had a world-class director promising to read our next script. And if he liked it, he would be able to get it made. But he was about to commit to directing another film, *Mary Reilly*. Our only hope was to get there first and knock it out. The clock was ticking . . .

Working in a feverish isolation, seven days a week, we cranked out our opus. Working on spec was a big gamble, since we didn't have the rights to Ed's life – if Tim hated the result, we would be stuck with a finished oddball script that would be extremely difficult to peddle, to put it mildly. So we tailored the screenplay to our perception of Tim's interests. Tim is completely intuitive, a completely personal filmmaker, and we wanted it to strike him on a gut level.

Both Tim and Ed used repertory companies of eccentric actors, and so we played up this angle. We introduced gothic visuals and bizarre locations whenever possible. But most importantly, we focused the story upon Ed's relationship with Bela Lugosi, since there were fascinating parallels with Tim's relationship with Vincent Price. Both Ed and Tim had worshipped the respective horror stars when they were young boys. Then they had met the actors and finally gotten to work with them at the end of their lives. This gave our movie an emotional foundation with which we felt Tim would empathize.

As we wrote, we were faced with huge choices. A man doesn't live his life in three acts. We had to look over Ed Wood's fifty-four years of existence, and find the story within that interested us.

First, we decided that most film biographies were boring. They seem compelled to follow the subject from cradle to grave. We felt this was too much to cover. Why is somebody's death important? The result often ends up quickly skimming the surface and being uninvolving. So we determined that we would only cover five years – the period that Ed was actually 'famous' for.

Then, as we examined the Ed/Bela relationship, an obvious three-act structure popped out. Page 10, they meet. End of act one, Ed makes his first film, using Bela's name. Act two, they struggle. End of act two, Bela dies. Act three, Ed has to figure out how to keep going, though Bela is gone.

Next was deciding what events to keep, and what to leave out. It was extremely important to us to be accurate and true to these people – yet many elements were dropped, for storytelling reasons. Ed's non-Lugosi projects were ignored. Bela's son and Bela's fifth and final wife were omitted. Two early Wood business partners, Alex Gordon and John Thomas, were left out. We had nothing against these people. But we wanted to focus on the Ed and Bela symbiotic bond, and these folks would have diluted that. These decisions seemed fair to our sense of biopic ethics.

Also, we avoided the bane of the genre: the 'composite characters'. All of Ed's scripted friends and extended family are real people. The beauty of Ed Wood's life is that truth literally *is* stranger than fiction. His story gave us the freedom to get away with absurdities that a normal screenplay never could. How could anyone complain the script was too wacky and bizarre? We could simply retort: It happened! Tor weighs 350 pounds and is bald. True! Ed wears his girlfriend's clothes. True! Bela wrestles a broken octopus. True! Ed's buddies get baptized in a swimming pool. All true!

As we started ordering the anecdotes which we found interesting, we were struck by a problem: we didn't know how Ed met anybody. These people were so obscure that the information had just fallen off the face of the earth. Even our principal source, Rudolph Grey's *Nightmare of Ecstasy*, a book of interviews with Ed's friends, didn't help. So we started inventing 'meet cutes' for most of the characters, as Ed accumulated his Magnificent Seven. As a sidenote, it's amusing to see how fabricated myth becomes fact – numerous magazine articles have since described how the real Ed Wood met Bela Lugosi in a mortuary, although we made up the entire thing.

We also compiled massive lists of Fun Facts. Every character had a page printout of random notations about the real person: funny things they had said and peculiar character traits. Then as we started writing a given scene, we would pull out each character's Fun Facts sheet. The goal became to cram in as much real information as we could: Ed wears dentures . . . Cameraman Bill is colorblind . . . Criswell bought his Cadillac from Mae West . . . At times, this data is overwhelming, but nobody can accuse the script of skimping on details. Also, this process often led to good drama. Bela revealing that he could have played Frankenstein, while in the middle of being humiliated in the octopus swamp, is a perfect example.

Finally, we had to figure out how to create a satisfying third-act climax and resolution. In a perfect world, *Glen or Glenda* would have been Ed Wood's final film – the man cranks out numerous silly monster movies, before learning his lesson, turning to personal honest film-making, and creating his autobiographical valedictory masterpiece.

But unfortunately, *Glen or Glenda* came first. So we had to turn *Plan 9 from Outer Space* into a climax. After much thought, the solution hit us, simple and elegant. The bad guys would become the Baptist moneymen, who want nothing more than a coherent film. All they are asking for is what any rational person would: continuity and logic. It is irony on top of irony. In the world of Ed, this impudence makes them villains. How dare they compromise him!

Then, to tie everything together, we invented one major fib. After establishing that Ed idolized Orson Welles (which he did), we made the two icons run into each other. The juxtaposition was ludicrous and thematically pleasing: both men were scrambling to raise money, shooting films haphazardly in pieces, and having their work recut by others. The greatest film-maker in the world and the worst film-maker in the world had landed in the same boat; they had identical problems. What greater way for Ed to have an epiphany then commiserating with the guy who made *Citizen Kane*?

After six weeks of writing, we had a 147-page script. This was substantially longer than the normal 120 – but we were afraid to cut anything, not knowing what Tim would respond to. Also, losing pages takes time, and we didn't have any. So, we took a gamble and handed him this epic first draft.

Tim received it on a Friday. On Sunday night, the phone rang: 'It's great. I'm gonna make it. And I don't want to change a word.'

Incredible. And he stayed true to his promise. Columbia Pictures acquired the project, and we never received a note from anybody. Then they lost interest when Tim decided to shoot in black-and-white, and Disney took over production. Still no notes. Then a start date became imminent, and finally the line producer began pleading for cuts, just to lower the schedule and budget. We looked at Tim, and he shrugged: *I* don't want to lose anything. But if you guys can find something . . .

As a reluctant sacrifice to the Gods, we cut Ed's shotgun wedding sequence, plus a couple other pages. We also simplified the locations. Then when Bill Murray joined the production, we juggled his lines a bit, for scheduling reasons. But other than that – no changes were done. Incredibly, Tim Burton had the courage and confidence to willingly shoot a first draft.

The movie is a huge tribute to a man who never achieved any recognition in his lifetime. But Ed Wood's glory was that he had integrity. He was never a Hollywood hack, indifferently creating 'product'. Ed put his soul on the line with every film – even when it wasn't necessary. When you watch his movies, you can feel the passion and personality of the guy behind the camera. If Ed's films fail on practically any barometer of artistic achievement, that's beside the point. The man was trying. It's a classic American success story: an eccentric individual achieves immortality, simply because he wouldn't bend to tradition.

October 1994

ED WOOD opened at the New York Film Festival in September 1994. The cast includes:

ED WOOD	Johnny Depp
BELA LUGOSI	Martin Landau
DOLORES FULLER	Sarah Jessica Parker
KATHY O'HARA	Patricia Arquette
CRISWELL	Jeffery Jones
REVEREND LEMON	G. D. Spradlin
ORSON WELLES	Vincent D'Onofrio
BUNNY BRECKINRIDGE	Bill Murray
GEORGE WEISS	Mike Starr
PAUL MARCO	Max Casella
CONRAD BROOKS	Brent Hinkley
VAMPIRA	Lisa Marie
TOR JOHNSON	George 'The Animal' Steele
LORETTA KING	Juliet Landau
ED REYNOLDS	Clive Rosengren
CAMERAMAN BILL	Norman Alden

Casting by	Victoria Thomas
Music by	Howard Shore
Costume Designer	Colleen Atwood
Editor	Chris Lebenzon
Production Designer	Tom Duffield
Director of Photography	Stefan Czapsky
Written by	Scott Alexander
	Larry Karaszewski

Based upon the book Nightmare of Ecstasy *by*	Rudolph Grey
Executive Producer	Michael Lehmann
Co-Producer	Michael Flynn
Produced by	Denise Di Novi
	Tim Burton
Directed by	Tim Burton

A Touchstone Pictures production.
Distributed by Buena Vista Distribution Inc.

xi

FADE IN:

EXT. HAUNTED MANSION – NIGHT

A haunted mansion sits up on a hill. A lightning storm rages furiously in the sky.

INT. HAUNTED MANSION PARLOR – NIGHT

We move through a spooky shrouded parlor. Thunder roars, and lightning flashes in the giant windows. In the center of the room lies an oak coffin.

Suddenly – the lid starts to creak open. A hand crawls past the edge . . . and then the lid slams up! Famed psychic CRISWELL *pops out. Criswell, forty, peers at us intently, his gleaming eyes framed under his striking pale blonde hair. He intones, with absolute conviction:*

> CRISWELL
> Greetings, my friend. You are interested in the unknown, the
> mysterious, the unexplainable . . . that is why you are here. So
> now, for the first time, we are bringing you the full story of what
> happened . . .
> *(extremely serious)*
> We are giving you all the evidence, based only on the secret
> testimony of the miserable souls who survived this terrifying
> ordeal. The incidents, the places, my friend, we cannot keep this a
> secret any longer. Can your hearts stand the shocking facts of the
> true story of Edward D. Wood, Junior??

EXT. NIGHT SKY

Lightning cracks.

We drift down past the dark clouds . . . through the torrential rain . . . and end up . . .

OPTICAL:

I

EXT. HOLLYWOOD – NIGHT

We've landed in Hollywood, 1952. We're outside a teeny, grungy playhouse. The cracked marquee proclaims ' "THE CASUAL COMPANY," WRITTEN AND DIRECTED BY EDWARD D. WOOD, JR.'

Pacing nervously in the rain is ED WOOD, *thirty, our hero. Larger-than-life, charismatic, confident, Errol Flynn-style handsome, Ed is a human magnet. He's a classically flawed optimist: sweet and well-intentioned, yet doomed by his demons within.*

The doors open, and Ed's pal JOHN 'BUNNY' BRECKINRIDGE, *forty-five, hurries out. Bunny is a wealthy, theatrical fop wearing a string of pearls.*

> BUNNY
> Ed, it's 8:15! We can't hold the curtain any longer.

> ED
> Damn, what am I gonna tell the cast? It's press night, and there's no press!

They turn to go *[– when a TEENAGER ON A BIKE *rides up. This pip-squeak drops his bike and hurries to the box office.*

> TEENAGE KID
> Sorry I'm late. My newspaper reserved a ticket for me, under the name 'Victor Crowley'.

Ed and Bunny glance at each other. Ed goes up to the kid.

> ED
> Hey you, what's going on here? Victor Crowley is an old man.

> TEENAGE KID
> Mr Crowley has the gout. So the paper assigned me to fill in.

Ed and Bunny grimace.]

INT. THEATER – LATER

There are only about five people in the audience. Filling other seats are buckets catching the rain.

* Cut from completed film.

2

On stage is a battlefield set, with a foxhole. Two stiff ACTORS *play weary World War II soldiers.*

ACTOR #1

Bill, do you believe in ghosts?

ACTOR #2

Nah, Tommy. That's just kiddie spook stories. Once you're dead, you stay dead.

ACTOR #1

I don't know, Bill. Out on that battlefield today, I saw this woman in white, floating above the dunes. Maybe it's just fatigue, or maybe it's the indignities of war, or maybe . . . it's something else.

BACKSTAGE:

Ed stands in the wings, mouthing every line with the actor.

***[*Suddenly the rest of the cast runs up, frantically upset. In a flowing white dress is* DOLORES FULLER, *twenty-three, a sharp hungry-for-a-career ingenue. She's near tears.*

DOLORES

Eddie, my dove just flew out of the window!

CREW MEMBER

She goes on in two minutes! What are we gonna do??

They all look to Ed, awaiting a response. He thinks a second, then excitedly claps his hands.

ED

Dolores, give me your shoes.

DOLORES

What?

ED

The ghost can be barefoot. *Give me your shoes!*

She hands Ed her white shoes. He snatches one, grabs a pair of scissors, and starts cutting up the shoe. Everyone is baffled. He keeps cutting the shoe . . . and it slowly takes on the shape of a dove!

* Cut from completed film.

3

Ed then grabs some pipe cleaners, works them into a shape, and sprints into the dressing room. He takes some green eye shadow and excitedly smears it on the pipe cleaners. Ed then hurries back out, jams the green pipe cleaners into the cut-up shoe . . . and it looks like a dove with an olive branch in its mouth!

The cast is flabbergasted.

CREW MEMBER

Wow.]

ONSTAGE:

The soldiers suddenly look up.

ACTOR #1

Hey, I think I see something!

Dolores floats down onto the stage, holding out the dove.

DOLORES

I offer you mortals the bird of peace, so that you may change your ways and end all this destruction.

CUT TO:

INT. SCRUFFY COFFEE SHOP — LATER THAT NIGHT

Ed and his gang celebrate opening night in a dirty twenty-four-hour diner. They're noisily slugging down drinks, in a big red booth.

ED

What a show! Everyone was terrific! Paul, your second-act monologue actually gave me chills.

He grins at Actor #1, aka PAUL MARCO, a young eager beaver who's loyal like a dog.

PAUL MARCO

Aw thanks, Eddie.

Actor #2, aka CONRAD BROOKS, a friendly, simple-minded lug, runs up waving a newspaper.

                              CONRAD
I got the early edition! It was just dropped off at the newsstand.

                               ED
                    (*he smiles at everyone*)
This is the big moment . . . !

Ed opens the paper to the entertainment page.

INSERT – THE NEWSPAPER:

Ed turns to a column, 'The Theatrical Life, By Victor Crowley'. Under this is a photograph of an old man with an ascot.

WIDE:

Everybody excitedly crowds around and starts reading. A moment . . . and then their faces drop. Clearly, this is a disastrous review. Their faces get sadder, and sadder . . . and then they finish. A melancholy beat, until –

                              BUNNY
What does that old queen know? He wasn't even there!
                    (*he knocks back a drink*)
Sending a copy boy to do his dirty work. Well *fuck him*!

                             DOLORES
Do I really have a face like a horse?

                           PAUL MARCO
What does 'ostentatious' mean?

Ed calmly waves his arms for attention. He tries to smile.

                               ED
Hey. Hey, it's not that bad. You just can't concentrate on the negative. He's got some nice things to say . . .
                     (*he scans the review*)
See, 'The soldier costumes are very realistic'. That's positive!

Everyone stares at their drinks, depressed. Ed launches into an upbeat speech.

                               ED
Hell, I've seen a lot worse reviews. I've seen ones where they

didn't even mention the costumes! Like, that last *Francis the Mule* picture – it got *terrible* notices. But it was a huge hit.

                    PAUL MARCO
Lines around the block.

                    ED
So don't take it too seriously. We're all doin' great work.

                    CONRAD
You really think so?

                    ED
Absolutely! It's just the beginning. I promise this: if we stick together, one day I'll make every single one of you famous.

He smiles at everyone at the table. They all believe what he says, and there is a hushed moment of dream-filled hope.

CUT TO:

INT. DOLORES' APARTMENT – LATE NIGHT

Ed and Dolores lie in bed, in the dark. He stares vulnerably at her.

                    ED
Honey, what if I'm wrong? What if I just don't have it?

                    DOLORES
Ed, it was only one review.

                    ED
Orson Welles was twenty-six when he made *Citizen Kane*. I'm already thirty!

                    DOLORES
Ed, you're still young. This is the part of your life when you're *supposed* to be struggling.

                    ED
I know . . . But sometimes I get scared this is as good as it's gonna get . . .

Dolores kisses Ed affectionately.

6

                    DOLORES
Things'll change for us. Nobody stays on the fringe forever.

She gets out of bed. We see her tiny apartment is drab and crumbling. Dolores turns on the shower, then walks to the closet. She looks inside.

                    DOLORES
God, where's my pink sweater? I can never find my clothes anymore . . .

ANGLE – ED:

He rolls over in bed, away from her.

    CUT TO:

INT. STUDIO WAREHOUSE – DAY

CU *on Ed reading* The Hollywood Reporter. *A* RUDE BOSS *in suspenders suddenly strides up.*

                    RUDE BOSS
Hey big shot, get off your ass. They need a potted palm over in the Carl Laemmle building.

                       ED
Sure thing, Mr Kravitz.

Ed jumps up. We widen, revealing he's in a giant greenhouse, packed with rows of potted plants and shrubs. Ed grabs a small palm tree and hurries out.

EXT. MOVIE STUDIO – DAY

Ed strolls across the busy movie lot, lugging the palm. He passes a soundstage and notices the stage door open a crack. Ed glances around, then puts down the palm and hurries in.

INT. SOUNDSTAGE – SAME TIME

A big-budget foreign-legion movie is shooting, with a huge cast and crew. A giant desert set has been erected, with camels and real sand dunes. Ed is blown away.

ED

Whoa, look at all this sand. This is real sand! My God, where'd they get all this sand?!*

A SECURITY GUARD *sees him.*

SECURITY GUARD

Hey, *you*! This is a closed set.

Ed is caught. He hurries out.

EXT. MOVIE STUDIO – DAY

Ed continues across the lot, carrying his palm tree. An OLD CRUSTY MAN *sticks his head out of an office window.*

OLD CRUSTY MAN

Hey, Eddie! Come in here. I got some great new stuff to show you.

Ed puts down the plant again and runs in.

INT. EDITING ROOMS – DAY

The old guy is proudly showing Ed stock footage on a moviola. The footage is totally random: giant explosions, buffalos stampeding, tanks, an octopus swimming, etc.

Ed is dazzled.

ED

This is fantastic! What are you gonna do with it all?

OLD CRUSTY MAN

Eh, probably file it away and never see it again.

ED

It's such a *waste*. If I had half a chance, I could make an entire movie out of this stock footage!
(*getting inspired*)
See, the story opens with these mysterious explosions. Nobody knows what's causing them, but it's upsetting all the buffalo. So the military is called in to solve the mystery.

* In the completed film, it was seeing the camels that caused Ed's amazed reaction.

OLD CRUSTY MAN

Ya forgot the octopus.

ED

No, I'm saving that for the big underwater climax!

The old guy cackles.

*[EXT. MOVIE STUDIO – DAY

Ed finally carries the tree into the Laemmle Building.]

INT. STUDIO OFFICES – SAME TIME

Young SECRETARIES *in June Cleaver hairdos are giggling.*

SECRETARY #1

They say he was a girl trapped in a man's body.

SECRETARY #2

I'll bet it hurt when they snipped his thing off.

EEWWW! All the girls shriek in horror. Ed walks in and puts down his plant.

ED

What are you ladies gabbin' about?

SECRETARY #1

You know that Christine Jorgensen freak? He/she/it's in *Variety.* Some producer is making a biopic.

ED
(startled)

R-really? I didn't see the story.

SECRETARY #1

Ah, it was buried in the back. The guy's a real small-time operator.

She holds up her Variety. *Ed hurriedly takes it.*

CUT TO:

* Cut from completed film.

9

INSERT – VARIETY:

The story headline says 'BOY-TO-CHICK FLICK TO CLICK'. We pull out, revealing we're now in:

INT. ED'S APARTMENT – DAY

Ed holds the newspaper while he paces around his apartment. The place has threadbare carpet, faded wallpaper, and an electric burner for a kitchen. A handful of mangy dogs run around. Tacked-up are movie posters for 'DRACULA', 'FREAKS', and 'THE MAGNIFICENT AMBERSONS'.

Dolores talks on the phone, while Ed silently coaches her.

> DOLORES
> *(on phone)*
> Yes, I've got Mr Edward Wood on the line. Could you please hold?

Ed gives her a thumbs up – perfect! He confidently takes the phone.

> ED
> Hello, Mr Weiss? I heard about your new project and was curious if you signed a director. Oh – you haven't? Well, if we could get together, I could explain why I'm more qualified to direct this than anyone else in town.
> *(beat)*
> Uh, I'd rather not go into it over the phone . . . Alright. Great! I'll see you then!

Ed hangs up and yelps excitedly. He kisses Dolores. She pulls away.

> DOLORES
> Eddie, I don't understand. Why are *you* the most qualified director for the Christine Jorgensen Story?

> ED
> *(nervous, he lies)*
> Aw, er, it's just a bunch of hot air. I had to say something to get in the door.

CUT TO:

INT. LOW-RENT HALLWAY – DAY

Ed walks jauntily along, wearing a snappy suit. He reaches a door that says 'SCREEN CLASSICS – George Weiss, President'. Ed fixes his hair, checks his clothes, then enters.

INT. SCREEN CLASSICS OFFICE – SAME TIME

It's a crowded room, piled with paperwork and files. Film cans are stacked everywhere, and framed one-sheets for 'TEST TUBE BABIES', 'BLONDE PICKUP' and 'GIRL GANG' litter the cracked walls. Sitting behind the messy desk is GEORGE WEISS, sixty, a rug merchant turned exploitation-film producer. He juggles a large sandwich and angrily barks into the phone.

> GEORGIE
> (*on phone*)
> Look, when I said you could have the western territories, I didn't mean *all eleven states*! I meant California, Oregon, and uh, what's that one above it . . . Washington. Oh really?! Well screw you!

Georgie slams down the phone. He smiles warmly at Ed.

> Can I help you?

> ED
> Yes, I'm Ed Wood. I'm here about directing the Christine Jorgensen picture.

> GEORGIE
> Yeah, well a couple of things have changed. It ain't gonna be the Christine Jorgensen story no more. Goddamn *Variety* printed the story before I had the rights, and now that bitch is asking for the sky.

> ED
> (*disappointed*)
> So you're not gonna make the movie?

> GEORGIE
> No, of *course* I'm gonna make the movie! I've already pre-sold Alabama and Oklahoma. Those repressed Okies really go for that twisted pervert stuff. So we'll just make it without that she-male.

We'll fictionalize it.

Georgie bites into his sandwich. Ed is dazed.

ED

Is there a script?

GEORGIE

Fuck no! But there's a poster.

Georgie pulls out artwork of a hermaphrodite: man on the left side, woman on the right. The lettering screams, 'I CHANGED MY SEX!'

It opens in nine weeks in Tulsa.

ED
(*mustering up his courage*)
Well, Mr Weiss, I'm your guy. I work fast, and I'm a deal: I write *and* direct. And I'm good. I just did a play in Hollywood, and Victor Crowley praised its realism.

GEORGIE

Hmm. There's five-hundred guys in town who can tell me the same thing. You said on the phone you had some kind of 'special qualifications'.

Ed takes a measured pause. This is his big revelation.

ED

Well, Mr Weiss, I've never told anyone what I'm about to tell you . . . but I really want this job.
(*he gulps*)
I like to dress in women's clothing.

GEORGIE

Are you a fruit?

ED

No, no, not at all! I *love* women. Wearing their clothes makes me feel closer to them.

GEORGIE

So you're not a fruit?

                              ED
Nah, I'm all man. I even fought in WW2.
                            (*beat*)
'Course, I *was* wearing ladies' undergarments under my uniform.

                           GEORGIE
You gotta be kiddin' me.

                              ED
Confidentially, I even paratrooped wearing a brassière and
panties. I'll tell ya, I wasn't scared of being killed, but I was
terrified of getting wounded, and having the medics discover my
secret.

Georgie sits back. It's a hell of a story.

                           GEORGIE
And this is why you think you're the most qualified to make my
movie?

                              ED
Yeah. I know what it's like to live with a secret, and worry about
what people are gonna think of you . . . My girlfriend still doesn't
know why her sweaters are always stretched out.

Georgie shrugs.

                           GEORGIE
Ed, you seem like a nice kid, but look around you . . .
                   (*he gestures at the posters*)
I don't hire directors with burning desires to tell their stories.
I make movies like *Chained Girls*. I need someone with experience
who can shoot a film in four days that'll make me a profit.
                            (*beat*)
I'm sorry. That's all that matters.

CUT TO:

INT. BAR – DAY

*Ed sits morosely in a scuzzy bar, three empty shot glasses in front of him.
A* BARTENDER *ambles over.*

BARTENDER
Are you gonna get something else?

Ed glumly empties his pocket. All he has is change. Ed sighs and staggers out.

EXT. HOLLYWOOD BOULEVARD – DAY

[Ed shuffles down the street, his head hanging low. A restaurant door opens, and an EISENHOWER-ERA NUCLEAR FAMILY exits. Whitebread Dad, Mom, Son and Daughter stride out in their starched clean clothes.

They march obliviously past Ed. He watches them go, then continues.] Ed reaches a building, 'HOLLYWOOD MORTUARY', and glances in the window. A pause, then he does a double-take.

THROUGH THE WINDOW:

The showroom is filled with sample coffins. Lying inside one is BELA LUGOSI.

ANGLE – ED:

He is flabbergasted.

INT. HOLLYWOOD MORTUARY – SAME TIME

Lugosi slowly sits up inside the coffin. Bela is a seventy-year-old man, once a great star, now a faded memory trying to hang on to his nobility. Quite frail and tired, he is still a master of the grand gesture.

An UNCTUOUS SALESMAN steps up. Bela speaks, in a thick Hungarian accent which gives him an Old World elegance.

BELA
Too constrictive. This is the most uncomfortable coffin I have ever been in.

SALESMAN
Gee, Mr Lugosi, I've never had any complaints before.

BELA
The selection is quite shoddy. You are wasting my time.

* Cut from completed film.

Mildly annoyed, Bela climbs out. He straightens his cloak and walks to the exit – where he bumps into nervous Ed.

> ED

Excuse me, Mr Lugosi??

> BELA
> (*irritated*)

I told you, I don't want any of your goddamn coffins.

> ED

No. I don't work here.

> BELA

Huh?

Bela peers at Ed, then glances confusedly over his shoulder at the salesman. Oh. Bela looks back at anxious Ed.

Who are you? What do you want?

> ED

I don't want anything. I'm just a really big, big fan. I've seen all your movies.

> BELA

Ha!

Bela strides out.

EXT. HOLLYWOOD BOULEVARD – SAME TIME

Bela hurries along. Ed chases after him.

> ED

Why were you buying a coffin?

> BELA

Because I'm planning on dying soon.

> ED
> (*concerned*)

Really?

> BELA

Yes. I'm embarking on another bus-and-truck tour of *Dracula*.

Twelve cities in ten days, if that's conceivable.

Bela pulls out a large smelly cigar and lights it.

> ED
>
> You know, I saw you perform *Dracula*. In Poughkeepsie, in 1938.

> BELA
>
> Eh, that was a terrible production. Renfield was a drunk!

> ED
>
> I thought it was great. You were much scarier in real life than you were in the movie.

> BELA
>
> Thank you.

> ED
>
> I waited to get your autograph, but you never came outside.

> BELA
>
> I apologize. When I play Dracula, I put myself into a trance. It takes me much time to re-emerge.

A city bus approaches.

> BELA
>
> Oh, there's my bus.
>   (*he checks his pockets*)
> Shit, where's my transfer?!

> ED
>
> Don't you have a car?

> BELA
>
> I refuse to drive in this country. Too many madmen.

The bus pulls up, and the doors open. Ed is worried he's about to lose his new friend. He gets an idea . . .

    CUT TO:

INT. 1948 NASH RAMBLER – DAY

Ed drives anxiously. Bela sits next to him, filling the car with smoke from

16

his big cigar.

ED

Boy, Mr Lugosi, you must lead such an exciting life. When is your
next picture coming out?

BELA

I have no next picture.

ED

Ah, you gotta be jokin'! A great man like you . . . I'll bet you have
dozens of 'em lined up.

BELA

Back in the old days, yes. But now – no one give two fucks for
Bela.

Bela puffs on his oversized cigar.

ED

But you're a big star!

BELA

No more. I haven't worked in four years. This town, it chews you
up, then spits you out. I'm just an ex-bogeyman.
(*he points*)
Make a right.

EXT. BELA'S NEIGHBORHOOD – DAY

*Ed drives past pumping oil wells and into a seedy neighborhood. They
reach a tiny, well-manicured house. Ed and Bela get out.*

BELA
(*bitter*)
They don't want the classic horror films anymore. Today, it's all
giant bugs, giant spiders, giant grasshoppers – who would believe
such nonsense!

ED

The old ones were much spookier. They had castles, full
moons . . .

BELA

They were *mythic*. They had a poetry to them.
> (*he lowers his voice*)

And you know what else? The women prefer the traditional monsters.

ED

The *women*?

BELA

The pure horror, it both repels and attracts them. Because in their collective unconsciousness, they have the agony of childbirth. The blood. The blood is horror.

ED

I never thought of that.

BELA

Take my word for it. You want to 'score' with a young lady, you take her to see *Dracula*.

Bela's eyes twinkle. He reaches his front door and unlocks it.

INSIDE:

It's awful. Squalid, dark, with skulls and strange voodoo objects scattered about. Up front hangs a large photograph of shockingly young Bela, handsome and regal.

Ed is stunned by this dismal place, but doesn't say anything. Within, dogs start barking crazily.

BELA

Ugh, what a mess.
> (*beat*)

My wife of twenty years left me last month. I'm not much of a housekeeper.

The dogs bark louder.

Shh! I'm coming! I will feed you!

ED

Well . . . I guess I should go. Perhaps we could get together again?

18

                    BELA
               (*he shakes his hand*)
Certainly. But now – the children of the night are calling me.

Bela smiles and steps inside. The door closes.

INT. DOLORES'S APARTMENT – DAY

Dolores is in her 1950s kitchenette, making a green jello mold. Ed bursts in, euphoric.

                    ED
Sweetie, you won't believe it! I've got the most incredible news!

                  DOLORES
                 (*excited*)
You got the job?!!

                    ED
Huh?!
                 (*confused*)
Oh, uh, no, I didn't get the job. But something *better* happened!

                  DOLORES
Better than not getting a job?

                    ED
Yeah! I met a movie star! Somebody *really big*!

                  DOLORES
Who? Robert Taylor?!

                    ED
                 (*annoyed*)
No! A horror movie star!

                  DOLORES
Boris Karloff!?

                    ED
Close! The *other* one!

                  DOLORES
You met Basil Rathbone!

                     19

ED

Oh, the hell with you. I met *Bela Lugosi!*

DOLORES

I thought he was dead.

Ed's eyes pop.

ED

No! He's very alive. Well . . . sort of. He's old, and frail – but he's still Bela Lugosi! And he's really nice.

DOLORES

Boy, I can't even remember the last time he was in a picture.

ED

It's a shame. He's such a great actor, and nobody uses him anymore.

DOLORES

So did you get his autograph?

Ed calms down. He smiles beatifically.

ED

No. It wasn't like that at all. It was just the two of us, and we were talkin' . . . and he treated me like – a friend . . .

CUT TO:

INT. STUDIO WAREHOUSE – DAY

Ed is back in the plant department, arguing with his boss.

RUDE BOSS

He's a *bum.*

ED

No, he's not! Do you realize how much money he made for this studio over the years? *Dracula! The Raven! The Black Cat!*

RUDE BOSS

Yeah? Well now he's a junkie. He don't deserve to work.

                              ED
That's not true –

                        RUDE BOSS
He's so great, *you* hire him.

                              ED
                        (*defensive*)
Well, uh, if I could I would . . .

The guy makes a mocking face and struts out. Ed glares.

CUT TO:

EXT. BELA'S HOUSE – NIGHT

It's Hallowe'en night. CHILDREN in trick-or-treating costumes parade up and down the streets. Through Bela's window, we see him and Ed watching television – a small fuzzy screen in a huge console.

INT. BELA'S HOUSE – SAME TIME

ON THE TV:

One of Bela's old 1930s horror films plays. Bela's evil character is hypnotizing somebody: his eyes stare the famous stare, then his hand does the famous hypnotic gesture.

ON ED AND BELA:

They are entranced. The men drink beers in silence. Bela's two dogs lie at his feet.

ON THE TV:

The old movie suddenly stops and VAMPIRA appears on the TV screen. Vampira, twenty-five, is the sexy 'Creature Feature' hostess, a pale ghoul slipped into a tight black dress.

She leers in front of a corny fog-shrouded set. There is a pumpkin, a broomstick and a sign reading 'HAPPY HALLOWE'EN'.

VAMPIRA
(*on TV*)

Ooo! Those eyes! He gives me the willies! The only thing scarier than him is this guy I dated last week: Charlie from Pittsburgh. Boy, talk about the living dead . . .

ON ED AND BELA:

Ed is disgruntled.

ED

Ugh! I hate the way she interrupts the pictures. She doesn't show 'em the proper respect.

BELA
(*glued to the TV*)

I think she's a honey. Look at those jugs.

Ed laughs. Bela waves his arm and starts doing his hypnotic hand gesture at the TV.

BELA

Vampira! You will come under my spell! You will be my slave of love.

ED
(*fascinated by Bela's hand*)

Hey Bela, how do you do that?

BELA

You must be double-jointed and you must be Hungarian.
(*back at the TV*)
Vampira, look at me! Stare into my eyes.

Ed joins Bela in this activity. The two of them wave their arms spookily at the TV.

Bela becomes fatigued.

I am getting tired. I need to take my medicine.

ED

Do you want me to get it for you?

BELA

No thank you, Eddie. I'll be alright.

Bela smiles. He gets up, shuffles across the room and steps behind a curtain. Ed is puzzled. Bela's thin arm appears and draws the curtain tight. We hear mysterious clanging, drawers opening and closing, and then silence.

Ed sits, waiting.

Behind the curtain, something drops. We hear a muffled 'Shit!'

Ed is getting worried. But then the curtain whips open, and Bela bounds out, grinning. He's a bundle of energy.

I feel better now.

AT THE DOOR:

The doorbell rings. Kids shout, 'Trick or treat!' Bela jumps up gleefully.

BELA

Children! I love children.

Bela puts on his famous cape, then gets a pair of fangs and sticks them in his mouth.

OUTSIDE:

Little kids in Lone Ranger and Howdy Doody costumes giggle expectantly.

Suddenly the door flies open, and standing there is Count Dracula! The real Count Dracula. YEOWWWW!!! The kids scream and run.

Bela chuckles. Every kid is gone . . . except one TOUGH BOY.

BELA

Aren't you scared, little boy? I'm going to drink your blood!

TOUGH BOY

Ehh, you're not a real vampire. You can't turn into a bat and those teeth don't frighten me.

Suddenly Ed lurches out, menacingly.

23

ED

Well how about *these teeth*?!!

Ed rips his teeth out of his head and thrusts them at the kid. The boy screams in terror and races away.

Bela is wowed.

BELA

Hey, how'd you do that?

Ed smiles impishly, then sticks the teeth back in his mouth.

ED

Dentures. I lost my pearlies in the war.

CUT TO:

*[EXT. STREET – LATER THAT NIGHT

Ed and Bela run towards us, Bela's cape flapping in the wind. Ed takes a swig from Bela's flask. They're a bit tipsy.

ED

Are you sure this is okay?

BELA

Don't worry. I do it every Hallowe'en.

EXT. CEMETERY – NIGHT

The moonlight shines down on a rickety old cemetery. The wind blows hauntingly and tombstones gleam in the blackness.

Ed and Bela reach the locked gates. They glance at each other, then start to climb over. Ed helps Bela. They jump down, and Ed peers nervously.

ED

Now what?

Bela looks like a child on Christmas morning. He takes another swig, then starts running giddily.

* Cut from completed film.

24

He disappears into the cemetery.

BELA

I am Dracula!

Bela darts happily through the graves.

His cape flies behind him.

I am the *bat*!!

Ed's eyes light up. He starts chasing after Bela.

Bela's heart is racing. He zig-zags past ancient crypts. Gargoyles peer down. The wind howls through the skeletal trees, silhouetted against the cloudy sky.

Ed runs through the shadows, trying to catch up.

Bela flaps his cape up and down. We almost think he's going to fly.

Ed races up, then quietly stops. He eagerly watches Bela, practically expecting him to turn into a bat. It's a magical, crazed moment.

I am *Dracula*! I will *live forever*!!!

Bela laughs, then lies down on the grass.

WIDE:

Ed slowly walks over and lies next to Bela. They're happy, eyes alert, on top of the world.

Ed peers in wonder at his new friend.

CUT TO:]

INT. SCREEN CLASSICS OFFICE – DAY

Ed sits across from Georgie. Ed's very excited.

GEORGIE

So what's the big news you couldn't tell me over the phone . . . again?

Ed gulps excitedly. He has a spiel all planned out.

ED

Mr Weiss, I was thinkin' about what you said, about how all your movies have to make a profit. And I realized, what's the one thing, that if you put in a movie, it'll be successful??

GEORGIE
(*he thinks*)

Tits.

ED

No. Better than tits – a *star*!

Georgie shakes his head.

GEORGIE

Eddie, you must have me confused with David Selznick. I don't make major motion pictures. I make crap.

ED

Yeah, but if you took that crap and put a star in it, you'd have something!

GEORGIE

Yeah. Crap with a star.

ED
(*impassioned*)

No! It would be something better! Something *impressive*. The biggest moneymaker you've ever had!

GEORGIE

Fine, maybe you're right. But it doesn't friggin' matter. I can't afford a star, so I don't even know what we're talking about.

Ed grins.

ED

What if I told you you could have a star for one thousand dollars?

GEORGIE
(*skeptical*)

Who?

Ed opens his valise and whips out an eight by ten glossy of Bela.

Lugosi?

ED

Yeah! *Lugosi!*

GEORGIE

Isn't he dead?

ED
(*annoyed*)

No, he's not dead! He lives in Baldwin Hills. I met him recently, and he wants to be in our picture.

GEORGIE

Our picture?

ED
(*sheepishly*)

Uh, yeah. Our picture.

Georgie mulls this over. He's interested.

GEORGIE

Why would Lugosi want to be in a sex-change flick?

ED

Because he's *my friend*.

Georgie stares carefully at Ed, then finally smiles.

GEORGIE

Alright, fine! You can direct it. I want a script in three days, and we start shooting a week from Monday.

ANGLE — ED:

He leaps up euphorically. He eagerly pumps George's hand.

ED

Thank you! Bless you, Mr Weiss! I promise I won't let you down!

CUT TO:

INT. ED'S APARTMENT — DAY

CU *on a Royal typewriter. Ed's hands whirl across the portable typewriter, frantically feeding in pages as fast as he can type. We pull out.*

Ed sits on the bed, typing. He's a blur of activity, juggling a cigarette,

27

coffee and a telephone, while he writes.

ED
(*on phone*)

But Bunny, you're perfect for this job! You're so good at organizing.

His adrenalin is pumping. Ed pours some booze into his coffee.

You know these people. I need all the transsexuals and
transvestites you can get.
(*he sucks on his cigarette*)

No, I don't care if they're not actors. I want realism. I want this
film to tell the *truth*! I've waited my whole life for this shot, and
I'm not gonna blow it.

*There's a knock at the door. Ed carries the phone on a long cord and
answers it. Bela hurries in, smiling broadly.*

BELA

Eddie, you got a new movie for me?!

ED

Yeah, it's gonna be a great picture! You'll love your character!
(*back into the phone*)

Bunny, Bela's here. Look, hit the bars, work some parties, and
get me transvestites! *I need transvestites!*

Ed hangs up and resumes typing. Bela is puzzled.

BELA

Eddie, what kind of movie is this?

ED

Well, it's about how people have two personalities. The side they
show to the world, and then the secret person they hide inside.

BELA
(*delighted*)

Oh, like Jekyll and Hyde! Ah, I've always wanted to play Jekyll
and Hyde! I'm looking forward to this production.

Ed stops typing. He pours Bela a drink.

ED

Ehh, your part's a little different. You're like the God that looks
down on all the characters, and oversees everything.

BELA

I don't understand.

ED

Well . . . you control everyone's fate. You're like the puppetmaster.

BELA
(*getting it*)

Ah, so I pull the strings!

ED

Yeah. You pull the strings –
(*he suddenly gets a look*)
'Pull the strings' . . . hey, that's pretty good!

Ed quickly starts typing again.

CUT TO:

INT. ED'S APARTMENT – NIGHT

Ed and Dolores sit at a card table, finishing up dinner. The dogs eat scraps below them.

ED

Wipe off your hands. I've got a little surprise for you . . .
(*he smiles nervously*)
I finished my script.

Ed anxiously pulls out a pile of pages. Dolores looks in awe at the cover: 'GLEN OR GLENDA by Edward D. Wood, Jr.'

DOLORES

Ed, I'm so proud! I'll read it as soon as I get home.

ED
(*apprehensive*)

Well, I'd really like to know what you think. Why don't you go in the bedroom and take a look at it? I'll wait . . .

There's an uneasy moment between them. She senses something funny. Dolores takes the script and goes into the bedroom. The door closes. Ed starts pacing . . .

DISSOLVE TO:

INT. BEDROOM – LATER

Dolores reads the script. She finishes the last page, then looks up. She is very shaken.

Dolores stands. She grabs the door and opens it.

THROUGH THE DOORWAY:

Ed stands somberly in drag. He's in a pantsuit, heels and pink angora sweater.

Dolores is totally rattled. She struggles for a response.

> DOLORES
> So *that's* where my sweater's been.

Ed silently nods.

> How long have you been doing this?

> ED
> Since I was a kid. My Mom wanted a girl, so she used to dress me in girlie clothing. It just kinda became a habit.

> DOLORES
> Jesus Christ! And you never told me?

> ED
> This is my way of telling you –

> DOLORES
> (*furious*)
> What, by putting it in a fuckin' script, for everyone to see?! What kind of sick mind would operate like that?

Ed is terribly hurt. Dolores shakes the script.

> And what about this so-called 'Barbara' character? It's obviously me! I'm so embarrassed! This is *our life*!

> ED
> (*quiet*)
> Of course it is. And that's why you should play the part.

30

                              DOLORES
  Oh! You got nerve, buddy.

He calmly points at the script.

                                ED
  It's a damn good role.

                              DOLORES
  That's not the issue!!
                         (*she suddenly stops.*)
  Ugh! How can you act so casual, when you're dressed like that?!

                                ED
  It makes me comfortable.

                              DOLORES
  Oh, just like the script!

Ed smiles serenely.

                                ED
  Exactly.
                          (*he takes her hand*)
  So what do ya say? Do you wanna break up . . . or do you wanna
  do the movie with me?

Dolores sighs.

  CUT TO:

INT. SCREEN CLASSICS OFFICE – DAY

The hallway is filled with eager TRANSVESTITES. *It's a very festive
atmosphere, and Bunny tries to create some order.*

                              BUNNY
  C'mon girls, simmer down! Let's have a professional atmosphere.
                     (*he stares down one* BLONDE)
  My Lord, you're a dead ringer for Peggy Lee!

Inside the office, Georgie angrily waves the script at Ed.

                             GEORGIE
  I thought this was gonna be a sex-change film!

                                31

> ED
> (*defensive*)

There's still a sex-change –

> GEORGIE

Yeah! Five pages right before it ends! The rest of the show is
about some schmuck who likes angora sweaters.

> ED

I don't think he's a schmuck.

> GEORGIE

And what's with this new title?! My poster says: 'I CHANGED MY
SEX'!

> ED

So change the poster. Trust me, you'll be better off. This is a story
that's gonna *grab* people.
> (*he goes into a pitch*)

It's about this guy. He's crazy about this girl – but he likes to wear
dresses. Should he tell her? Should he not tell her? He's torn.
George, this is *drama*.

Georgie throws up his hands.

> GEORGIE

Fine, shoot whatever baloney you want! I give up. Just make sure
it's seven reels long.

CUT TO:

EXT. STREET – EARLY MORNING

We are on location for Ed's first film! A SMALL CREW *of a dozen unpack
the camera and reflectors from their cars. Ed's voice rises above the
hubbub.*

> ED
> (*off*)

Excuse me, could I have everyone's attention?! Could you gather
around? I've got something to say.

The crew members put down their things and gather in a circle. In the middle, we reveal Ed, in complete drag. Dress, nylons, pumps, lovely blonde wig . . . he's quite a sight. Like an eager Scoutmaster, he addresses his troops.

Everybody, we're about to embark on quite a journey. Four days of hard work . . . but when it's over, we'll have a picture that'll entertain, enlighten, and maybe even move millions of people.

*[Two GRIPS glance at each other.

Now the only way we're gonna achieve all this is if we stay on schedule. Day One – *today* – we'll start easy. We have eighteen silent scenes that can be shot quickly: cars parking, Patrick's suicide, me strolling as a man, me strolling as a woman, etc.
                    (*beat*)
After lunch, we'll bring in the Inspector and the Doctor. The Doctor is very important to the plot, so we might have to spend time on retakes. But it's worth it. Scene totals for the first day is thirty-four.
                (*he catches his breath*)
Day Two, we'll be a little busier –]

Veteran CAMERAMAN BILL, *an old guy with thick glasses, speaks.*

CAMERAMAN BILL
Excuse me Eddie, I don't mean to interrupt . . . but I'm gettin' a little worried about the light.

He points up. Everybody looks at the sky.

Ed nods in agreement.

ED
Good thinkin'. We'll talk about Days Three and Four later. Now let's get that first shot off. It's Scene seventeen, Glenda looking into a window.

[The crew disperses. Ed quickly runs in his heels over to the burly make-up man HARRY.

ED
Okay, do I need any touch-up?

*Cut from completed film.

33

MAKE-UP MAN HARRY

I'm telling ya, eyelashes are the way to go.

ED
(*irritated*)

Harry, we've discussed this a million times. I don't want to look like a girl. I want to look like myself.

MAKE-UP MAN HARRY
(*disgruntled*)

Fine. Then you look *beautiful*.

Harry humorlessly powders Ed's nose. Ed turns away and suddenly shouts into the giant megaphone.

ED

Places, everyone! Roll camera!

CAMERAMAN BILL
(*nonchalant*)

Rolling.]

WIDE:
Ed chucks the megaphone and runs crazily past the camera and behind a building.

ED'S VOICE

and – *action!*

A pause, and then Ed, in character as Glenda, calm and dignified, steps out and walks down the sidewalk.

Ed stops at a store window. He's totally in shadow.

A grip grimaces. He turns on a light.

Ed lights up. He looks in the window, admires a dress on display, then silently walks out of frame.

A beat. Ed screams.

ED

And, *cut!* Print it! Let's move on!

CAMERAMAN BILL

Don't you want a second take, for protection?

ED
(*exhilarated*)
What's to protect? It was perfect!

Suddenly a police car turns the corner.

CREW MEMBER
Cops!

ED
We don't have a permit. *Run!*

Everyone grabs equipment and takes off.

WIPE TO:

INT. LARCHMONT STUDIOS — DAY

The company is now shooting inside a dinky soundstage. There are dirty mattresses tacked on the walls. They prep Bela's set: a fishnet-draped armchair in front of a flat. Ed is perched high in his director's chair, back in men's clothes.

*[ED
The set doesn't look right! It looks too . . . empty. Clutter it up. Put a skeleton in the corner. And what's that thing over there?

PAUL MARCO
I don't know.

ED
Well, it looks good. Let's use it!

Georgie hurriedly strides over. He holds the script.

GEORGIE
Ed! What's with these revised pages?! A scene in a smelting factory? A buffalo stampede?? *Three-hundred soldiers storming Anzio Beach??!* What's going on here? I can't afford to film this nonsense!

ED
Don't worry. We're not gonna film any of it.

* Cut from completed film.

GEORGIE

Then how's it gonna get in the picture?!

ED

I know a guy in Universal's stock house – he's giving me the
footage for free. This movie's gonna look like a million bucks.

Georgie nods: oh, okay.]

VOICE
(*off*)

Mr Lugosi has arrived!

Ed jumps excitedly.

ED

Oh my God!
(*he yells*)
Mr Lugosi is here! Now everyone, when he walks on the stage –
(*nobody is listening, so Ed uses his megaphone*)
Now everyone, when he walks on the stage, treat him normal. I
know Bela Lugosi is a world-famous star, and you're all a little
excited, but we're professionals. So if you treat him with respect,
everything will be alright.

AT THE STAGE DOOR:

*The door swings open, and Bela strides in, looking dapper. He glances at
the teensy stage, and his face falls imperceptibly.*

Ed runs up, bounding with enthusiasm.

ED

Bela! It's great to see you!
(*he glances at his watch*)
And eight o'clock on the dot. Right on time!

BELA

I am always on time.

ED

Of course! Well, we got a big day planned for you. First, we're
gonna start off a little easy, with you in that armchair over there.
Then, once you're up to speed and cooking, we'll reset and bring

36

out the laboratory equipment –

> BELA
> (*he leans in and whispers*)
> Um, Eddie, do you have my money?

> ED
> Huh?! Oh yeah, of course.

Ed and Bela step over to a corner.

ACROSS THE ROOM:

From a distance, Ed pulls a wad of money from his pocket and peels off a few bills for Bela. The crew watches, fascinated.

WIPE TO:

INT. LARCHMONT STUDIOS – LATER

Bela is seated in the ratty armchair on the set. Harry does his make-up. Harry glances at Bela's arm, and it is full of track marks. Harry grimaces, but doesn't say anything.

Conrad eagerly scurries up.

> CONRAD
> Mr Lugosi, I know you're very busy, but could I have your autograph?

> BELA
> (*cordial*)
> Of course.

Conrad hands him a copy of the script. Bela signs it.

> CONRAD
> You know which movie of yours I love, Mr Lugosi? *The Invisible Ray*. You were great as Karloff's sidekick.

Bela's face suddenly hardens. He snaps.

> BELA
> 'Sidekick'?? 'Karloff'?!! Fuck you!! Karloff doesn't deserve to smell my shit! That limey cocksucker can rot in hell, for all I care!!!

WIDE:

Ed panickedly runs up.

> ED
>
> What happened? Jesus, Connie, what did you do?

> CONRAD
> *(upset, close to crying)*
>
> Nothin'! I told him he was great.

> BELA
>
> How dare that asshole bring up Karloff?!! You think it takes talent to play Frankenstein?! *No!* It's just make-up and grunting! *Grrr! Grrr! Grrr!*

Ed is frozen in fear. He glances across the stage.

Georgie is flabbergasted. He points urgently at his watch.

Ed nods. He motions to Conrad: get out of here. Conrad runs away. Ed leans in to Bela.

> ED
>
> You're right, Bela. Now Dracula, *that's* a part that takes acting.

> BELA
>
> Of course! Dracula requires *presence*. It's all in the voice, and the eyes, and the hand –

Bela waves his outstretched arm. Ed tries to calm him.

> ED
>
> Look, you seem a little agitated. Do you maybe wanna take a little break, go for a nice walk . . . and then we'll come back and shoot the scene?

> BELA
>
> *Bullshit!* I am ready now! Roll the camera!!

The crew is baffled. Ed shrugs at them.

> ED
>
> Um, okay . . . roll camera.

CAMERAMAN BILL
(*unsure*)
Rolling.

ED
Sound!

SOUNDMAN
Speed.

CAMERA ASSISTANT
Mark. Scene thirty-one.

The Assistant claps the slate in front of Bela, then runs.

ED
And . . . action?

It's dead quiet. Nobody knows what's about to happen. We move into Bela. And . . . he suddenly assumes character. Like the consummate pro he is. Bela gets a wicked, sinister leer, then starts intoning threateningly:

BELA (*as the* SPIRIT)
'Beware. Beware! Beware, of the big green dragon that sits on your doorstep. He eats little boys! Puppy dog tails! Big fat snails! Beware. Take care. Beware!'

CU — ED:

He is blown away. He quietly mumbles in amazement.

ED
Cut. Perfect.

WIPE TO:

INT. STAGE — NEXT DAY

Dolores studies her script, as the crew lights a flimsy kitchen set. Ed strolls past, nonchalantly removing a ladies' wig and earrings. She stares in disbelief.

DOLORES
How can you just walk around like that, in front of all these people?

ED
Hon', nobody's bothered but you.

39

(*he gestures*)
Look around – they couldn't care less.

                    DOLORES
Ed, this isn't the real world! You've surrounded yourself with
weirdos!

                    ED
Say it a little louder. I don't think Bela heard you.

Dolores quiets down. She feels bad.

Dolores. I need your help . . .

WIPE TO:

INT. FILMING IN PROGRESS – LATER

*A scene is being shot, oncamera. Ed (as Glen) and Dolores (as Barbara)
stare into each other's eyes. He's dressed normal and she wears a fuzzy
angora sweater.*

                    ED (*as* GLEN)
'My mind's in a muddle. I thought I could stop wearing these
things. I tried, honestly I tried . . .'

                    DOLORES (*as* BARBARA)
                    (*tentative*)
'Glen, I don't fully understand this. But maybe together – we can
work it out.'

*She stands up, dramatically takes off her angora sweater, and gives it to
Ed.*
He holds it meaningfully, then smiles proudly.

                    ED
Music swells . . . and *cut* and *print it*.

Ed and Dolores hug.

CUT TO:

*[INT. EDITING ROOM – DAY

ON A MOVIOLA:

We see the black-and-white image of Dolores taking off her angora and giving it to Ed.

We pull out. Ed and Georgie are hunched over, watching the movie. Ed smiles proudly.

> ED
>
> And we fade out. 'The End.'
> > (*The film runs out*)
> What do you think?

Georgie peers at his watch. He shakes his head.

> GEORGIE
>
> I think it's fifty-seven minutes long.

> ED
>
> Yeah? Whatever. So did you like it?

> GEORGIE
> > (*like a lecturing teacher*)
> Ed, what was the one thing I asked you to do? Make it *seven reels long*. I've got contracts with my exhibitors. If it ain't over an hour, they won't play it.

> ED
>
> Gee, I used every frame of film we shot. Maybe they won't notice.

> GEORGIE
>
> They'll notice.
> > (*beat*)
> Look, why don't you let me take over from here? I can do a few tricks: pad it out with more stocks footage, add establishing shots. . .

> ED
>
> Um, I guess –

> GEORGIE
>
> Good. And one more thing. I think your 'Written, Directed and Starring Ed Wood' credit is a bad idea.

*Cut from completed film.

41

                              ED

Why?! I did all those things! Hell, I even built the props.

                            GEORGIE

And you did a bang-up job, too. But you don't want other
producers to know that's you in drag. Trust me. It's a career
killer.

Ed is quite upset.

                              ED

But I'm proud. I wrote, directed, and starred in it – just like
Orson Welles in *Citizen Kane*!

                            GEORGIE

Yeah?? Well Orson Welles didn't wear angora sweaters, did he??!

Ed is beaten.

   CUT TO:

INT. SCREENING ROOM – NIGHT

*It's the cast and crew screening! The eager two-dozen people are packed
into a tiny screening room.*

*The lights dim, and the movie starts. A library music fanfare, and then:
'Bela Lugosi in* GLEN OR GLENDA*'*

Everyone applauds excitedly. Bela smiles.

Credits continue: 'Featuring Daniel Davis and Dolores Fuller'

The audience is baffled. Bunny blurts out.

                            BUNNY

   Daniel *who*?!

Dolores leans in to Ed.

                           DOLORES

Ed, who is Daniel Davis?

                              ED
                            (*sour*)
Some weirdo who likes to wear dresses.

                              42

DISSOLVE TO:

INT. SCREENING ROOM – LATER

ONSCREEN:

Dolores looks tenderly at Ed.

> ### DOLORES
> 'Glen. Is it another woman?'

Ed as Glen nervously ponders his response.

But suddenly – music thunders in. The movie cuts to buffalo stampeding. Bela's angry face is superimposed over this .

> ### BELA
> (*on screen*)
> 'Pull the string! Pull the string!'

IN THE AUDIENCE:

People are impressed by this technique. Bela nods in approval.

ONSCREEN:

Out of nowhere, cheap jazz music starts, and the movie abruptly cuts to sleazy stag party-style footage! A bare-chested man whips a bound woman! A woman dominates another tied to a large stick! A brunette violently rips off her dress and does a hoochie-coochie dance!

IN THE AUDIENCE:

The crowd is stunned.

> ### CAMERAMAN BILL
> I didn't shoot that!

Ed looks back at Georgie, who's wearing a big satisfied grin.

> ### ED
> Georgie, what's with the stag footage?? You said you were cutting in *establishing shots*.

> ### GEORGIE
> I did. I established some tits and ass.

Ed rolls his eyes. He turns back to the movie.

INT. PARTY – LATER THAT NIGHT

Everybody is celebrating, with a raucous party. People are boozing it up. Big band music plays. Ed dances with Dolores. Paul smokes a joint. Conrad falls over a table and breaks a lamp. Bela dances happily with a cute young REDHEAD.

> BELA
> Wasn't I something . . .? Did you see how I command the screen?!

Ed's giddy buddies stumble over with foaming glasses of beer.

> BUNNY
> Ed, it was superb.

> CONRAD
> A great show. A little strange . . . but great – especially my scenes.

> ED
> Just like I always promised. Now you're among the immortals. You're movie stars.

> PAUL MARCO
> *(he raises his glass)*
> Here's to Ed. For making us into something.

It's a warm moment. They all clink their glasses.

Dolores kisses Ed.

CUT TO:

EXT BUNGALOW HOUSE – DAY

We're outside a cute little Spanish bungalow house. Ed and Dolores are moving in. They lug furniture from a rented truck.

> ED
> From today on, our lives are different! We'll be swimming laps in the same pool Jean Harlow did.

DOLORES

I don't know. It's so much money . . .

ED

Who cares?! We're on a *roll*! These are the moments in life you're supposed to grab.

DOLORES

But Ed, we're not even married. And you don't have a job.

ED

But *you* do! And anyway, I've got tons of new scripts. And now that I have a track record, studios are bound to hire me!

She just stares. Ed shrugs, semi-reassuringly.

ED

Look on the bright side. If we miss the rent, what's the worst they can do?

DOLORES

Toss us out on our ass.

ED

Exactly.

INT. BUNGALOW – DAY

The house is moved in. Ed's unkempt dogs run about. Pumped-up Ed sits on the bed, typing fiendishly fast while wearing an angora sweater. A cigarette dangles from his mouth and a bottle of booze lays in his lap. Bela sits quietly nearby.

ED

How 'bout a western? People love westerns.

BELA

Mm, I don't like horses. Do I have to get on one?

ED

Eh, forget it. What else is big?
(*his face lights up*)
Teenagers! Jailbait pics! Yeah . . . You got the juvenile delinquent, his girlfriend from the wrong side of the tracks –

BELA

Who do I play?

ED

Uh, a cop. *No!* You play the father. He's *angry!* He doesn't like
seeing his son – no – he doesn't like seeing his *daughter* behave this
way!

BELA
(*cautious, not to offend*)

Well . . . can't *I* play the romantic part? I'm tired of always being
the bad guy. You know, back in Hungary, I played Romeo! I would
like to be the lover again – me, in a boat, with the girl . . .

Ed considers this.

ED

Sure. Romance, that's great! To engineer your comeback, we're
gonna need a whole slate of pictures. Once *Glen or Glenda* takes off,
we'll slam you into one, then another then another!

BELA
(*he smiles*)

That's good. I could use the money.

ED

But we need to start off with a bang! Something we *know* the
audience will want to see. Hmm. What was your biggest hit?

BELA
(*he thinks*)

Hmm . . . my biggest hit? That would probably be *Dracula*.

ED

Of course!

Ed grabs a pen and excitedly scrawls out the word 'DRACULA'. *Bela frowns.*

BELA

Those bastards at Universal. I made so much money for them, and
now I can't get the time of day.

ED

So let's make another *Dracula*. Let's make *The Return of Dracula!*

                          BELA
We can't. Those sons-of-bitches control the rights.

                          ED
They do? Shoot. There *must* be a way to get round that . . .

Ed's mind is working. He holds out the paper and stares at it. Suddenly, he grins. He grabs the pen and makes a period after the 'DR' *It now says* 'DR. ACULA.'

Ha ha! Dr Acula!

                          BELA
Dracula?

                          ED
No! *Doctor Acula*! You can still wear the cape, have the fangs . . . but you're a doctor! Not a count.

                          BELA
Ah! This is very exciting.

                          ED
                       (*inspired*)
I gotta type this up, while it's still fresh!

Ed rips the paper from his typewriter, puts in a blank page, and starts typing.
CUT TO:]

EXT. MOVIE STUDIO GATE – DAY

We're outside the imposing gates of MGM. The lion logo is overhead. Ed drives up in his dirty Nash Rambler convertible. He wears his nicest suit. Ed peers nervously at the GUARD.

                          ED
Excuse me, I'm here to see Mr Feldman.

The Guard stares suspiciously at Ed. His filthy car is leaking oil.

                          GUARD
What's your name?

                          ED
Edward D. Wood, Junior.

The man frowns. He looks through his files – then finds a parking slip with Ed's name. He is surprised.

> GUARD
> Oh. Eh, he's in the Executive Building. You can park in the reserved section.

Ed smiles.

*[INT. EXECUTIVE WAITING ROOM – DAY

The room is very posh, with fancy paneling and marble floors. Ed sits nervously under posters for 'GRAND HOTEL' and 'QUO VADIS.' Film cans labled 'Glen or Glenda' rest in his lap.

> SECRETARY
> Sir, Mr Feldman will see you now.

She hits an electric button. A large oak door swings open.]

INT. OFFICE – DAY

Behind a giant desk is MR FELDMAN, a glib, thin, over-caffeinated man. He jumps up, smiling.

> MR FELDMAN
> Mr Ward, it's a delight to meet you.

> ED
> *(shaking his hand)*
> It's Wood. Ed Wood.

> MR FELDMAN
> Wood? Ward? Wood.
> *(puzzled, he glances at his appointment book)*
> Hey, what do you know. It *is* Wood. Dang secretaries, you can never get a good one. Right?

Ed shrugs. Feldman grins.

> MR FELDMAN
> So what are you bringing me? Looks like you got some film cans.

* Cut from completed film.

48

ED

Well Mr Feldman, some people have resumés to show. I've got my own movie.

MR FELDMAN

Really?! Well, good for you.

ED

I just made this picture, over at Screen Classics. It opens next week.

MR FELDMAN

Screen Classics? Hmm, don't know them.

ED

Nobody in town has seen it, so I'm givin' you first crack at my talents.

MR FELDMAN

I can't wait to take a look.
                    (*he claps his hands*)
So what's up next?

Ed leans in.

ED

Well, Mr Feldman, I don't believe in thinking small. So I've got a whole slate of pictures for you: *The Vampire's Tomb*, *The Ghoul Goes West* . . . and *Doctor Acula*!

MR FELDMAN

Doctor Acula? I don't get it.

ED

Dr Acula!

Ed writes it out, 'DR. ACULA, *then waves it in Feldman's face. Feldman nods.*

MR FELDMAN

Oh, 'Dr Acula.' I get it.
                    (*beat*)
I don't like it.

ED

But Bela Lugosi's in it!

MR FELDMAN

Lugosi's washed-up. What else you got?

49

Ed grimaces. Lugosi was 90 per cent of his pitch. He vamps.

> ED
>
> Well . . . I've got another project I wasn't gonna tell you about. Lugosi's in it, but he's got a smaller part. The lead is an ingenue, a sterling young actress named Dolores Fuller. The title is *Bride of the Atom.*

> MR FELDMAN
>
> Ah! Atomic Age stuff, huh? I like it.
> > *(he smiles)*
>
> I'll tell you what, Mr Wood. Why don't you leave those film cans, and my associates and I will take a look at your little opus. Maybe we can do business together.

Ed is elated.

INT. STUDIO SCREENING ROOM – DAY

Feldman and his fellow SMARMY EXECUTIVES *sit in a plush screening room. They are viewing* Glen or Glenda.

ONSCREEN:

Ed is in drag. A SOLEMN NARRATOR *within the movie speaks:*

> SOLEMN NARRATOR
> > *(voiceover)*
>
> 'Give this man satin undies, a dress, and a sweater . . . and he's the happiest man in the world. He can work better, think better, even play better – and be more of a credit to his community and his government.'

ANGLE ON THE EXECUTIVES:

They are stupefied. Yikes!

> EXECUTIVE #1
>
> What the hell is this?!

> EXECUTIVE #2
>
> Is this an actual movie?!

> EXECUTIVE #1
>
> It can't be.

It's fuckin' ridiculous!

Feldman squints at the screen.

MR FELDMAN
Wait a minute. That guy in the dress – he's the one I met with
today! This must be a big *put-on*!
(*he chuckles*)
It's probably another one of Billy Wellman's practical jokes!

Everybody suddenly starts howling with laughter.

CUT TO:

EXT. NEWSSTAND – DAY

Ed zooms up and chipperly jumps from his car. He buys a Los Angeles
Herald-Express, *eagerly opens it to the entertainment pages . . . and then
gets a confused look. Ed quickly starts riffling through the pages –
something is wrong.*

EXT. PHONE BOOTH – DAY

Ed angrily shouts into the phone.

ED
Georgie, what happened?! I thought *Glen or Glenda* was opening
next week! Where's the ads?

*[OLD-FASHIONED SPLIT SCREEN:]

Georgie appears on the phone.

GEORGIE
(*pissed-off*)
'Where's the ads?'! The ads are in Alabama, Indiana and
Missouri! You schumuck, it ain't gonna play LA!

ED
Why not??

* This device not used in completed film.

GEORGIE

*[Because I can't sell it to save my life! You made a goddamn
feathered fish. Is it an art film, a horror show, a hygiene flick?
Nobody knows! I'm beggin' people to book it.

ED
(*insulted*)
Maybe it needs special handling.

GEORGIE

Screw you, Wood! I even sunk more money into different titles:
Transvestite, He or She?, I Led Two lives . . . it *doesn't matter*!]
Nobody wants to see the piece of shit.

ED

You can't talk that way about my movie.

GEORGIE

'Your movie'?! I wish it was your movie! I wish I hadn't blown
every dime I ever made into this stinkbomb. If I ever see you
again, I'll kill you!!!

*Georgie slams down the phone. His split screen wipes off, leaving Ed
standing alone.*

Ed stares at the phone, then quietly hangs it up.

CUT TO:

INT. OLYMPIC AUDITORIUM — NIGHT

Wham! A WRESTLER *throws another* WRESTLER *at the mat. The crowd
cheers raucously. We're at the Saturday Night Wrestling Matches!*

*In the stands are Ed, Dolores and Bunny. Seated around them are
hollaring truckers and ex-Marines. Bunny giggles and nudges gloomy Ed.*

BUNNY
So guess where I'm going next weekend?

ED

I don't know. Where?

* Cut from completed film.

52

BUNNY

Mexico! And guess what I'm going to do there?!

ED
(*not enjoying this game*)
I dunno. Lie on the beach?

BUNNY
Wrong! I'm getting my first series of hormone shots! And once those babies kick in, they're gonna remove my organs, and *make me a woman!*

Ed is astonished.

ED

Jesus! Are you serious?

BUNNY
Yes! I've dreamed of it for years, but your movie made me realize I've got to take action. *Goodbye, penis!*

The nearby truckers stare. Dolores covers her face.

DOLORES
Shh! Will you keep it down?

The crowd suddenly roars and jumps up. A favourite wrestler has entered the ring, massive TOR JOHNSON, *fifty. Tor is an incredible sight: a bald, lumbering behemoth.*

RING ANNOUNCER
(*amplified*)
Now entering the ring, in the gold trunks, 350 bone-crunching pounds of pure strength, the 'Swedish Angel' . . . Tor Johnson!!!

The crowd goes apeshit. The stands are going to collapse from the shouting.

Ed's eyes are the size of saucers.

ED
My God, look at that guy. He's a mountain!

The bell rings. Tor quickly grabs his OPPONENT, *a man in a blue mask and throws him at the ground. Then Tor jumps onto his stomach, easily picks him up and heaves him at the ropes.*

53

People cheer. Ed is flabbergasted.

> ED
>
> I've never seen anything like him!

> BUNNY
>
> And once I'm a woman, Jean-Claude and I are getting married. I'll be a June bride –

> ED
> (*eyes glued to the ring*)
>
> Shh! He's so big! He's a *monster*! Can you imagine what that guy would be like in a movie?

ON TOR:

He screams maniacally in Swedish. Tor lifts the Opponent over his head and tosses him into the stands. Three rows of chairs get knocked over.

CUT TO:

*[EXT. WRESTLERS' BAR – NIGHT

A tiny miniature European car pulls up. Tor Johnson is squeezed inside – ludicrously oversized for this vehicle. Tor carefully wedges himself out and enters the bar.]

INT. WRESTLERS' BAR – SAME TIME

This rowdy bar is packed with burly WRESTLERS. *Tor walks in, and men cheerily yell out: 'Hey, Tor!' 'Hi, Tor!' Tor grins. In person, he actually seems a jolly, outgoing fellow.*

Ed waves from the corner.

> ED
>
> Mr Johnson, over here!

Tor smiles and lumbers over.

> Glad you could fit me in your schedule.

----

* Cut from completed film.

TOR
(in a hoarse Swedish accent)

Da pleasure be mine.

They shake hands. Ed's hands look like a baby's in Tor's giant mitts.

Tor tries to sit in the booth. But he can't fit.

TOR

Could we moovf to table?

ED

Oh, of course!

Ed jumps up. They move to a large table. Now Tor is happy. He starts shoveling beer nuts into his mouth.]

*So, Mr Johnson –

TOR

Tor!

ED

Tor. Have you ever thought about becoming an actor?

TOR
(he chuckles)

Mm, not good-lookink enough.

ED

I think you're quite handsome.

TOR

No. With hair, yah. But I must shave head for wrestlink. It scare da crowds. Dey like that.

Ed smiles.

ED

Well, I think you'd be a sensation in pictures.

TOR

But what bout accent? Some people tink I haf too much accent.

---

* In the completed film this scene took place in Tor's dressing room; the dialogue was adjusted to suit the different location.

ED

Nah, that doesn't matter! It's a visual medium.

A WAITRESS *saunters over.*

WAITRESS

Tor, what can I get ya?

TOR

I'll haf eight beers.

WAITRESS
(*nonchalant, to Ed*)

And you?

ED

Uhh, I'll have just one.

She walks off. Tor shakes the now-empty nut bowl.

TOR

And more nuts!

Ed tries to grab Tor's attention.

ED

So anyway, I've got this new script, *Bride of the Atom,* and there's a part you're ideal for: 'Lobo.' He's tough. A brute. But he has a heart – and at the end he saves the girl.

TOR
(*he laughs merrily*)

I like. When do movie shoot?

ED

Hopefully, very soon. I'm just awaiting the final okay from Mr Feldman at MGM.

CUT TO:

INT. ED AND DOLORES'S BEDROOM – LATE NIGHT

Ed and Dolores are asleep. Suddenly the phone rings. Ed fumbles for it and groggily answers.

ED

Ed Wood Productions . . .

We hear Bela's weak voice.

BELA
(*on phone*)

Eddie . . . help me . . .

ED

Bela?

BELA
(*on phone*)

Eddie . . . please come over –

Click. The phone hangs up. Ed is very alarmed.

EXT. BELA'S HOUSE – LATE NIGHT

The wind is blowing. Ed's Nash roars up, and he jumps out, a coat over his pajamas. He runs up and pounds on Bela's door.

ED

Bela?!

Ed tries the door. It's unlocked.

INT. BELA'S HOUSE – SAME TIME

Ed steps into the dark room, and is stunned by what he sees: Bela is slumped on the floor, pasty white, eyes glazed. A rubber tube is tied on his arm, and a hypodermic needle lies next to him.

The dogs crouch behind him, whimpering. Bela looks up through despondent, half-opened eyes.

BELA

Eddie . . . my friend.

Aghast, Ed runs over.

ED

Bela, what happened?!

I didn't feel well . . .

ED

Let me take you to the hospital.

BELA

No hospital. Just take me to the couch . . .

Ed nods. He picks up the old man and carries him across the room to the couch. The large portrait of Bela, young and robust, peers down.

ED

Should I call a doctor?

BELA

Nah. This happens all the time . . .

Ed puts a pillow under Bela's head.

ED

Is there anything I can get you? Water? A blanket?

BELA

Goulash.

ED
(*distressed*)

I don't know how to make goulash.

Ed sits next to him. An awkward pause.

What's in the needle?

BELA

Morphine, with a demerol chaser.
(*he starts crying*)
Eddie, I'm so broke. I don't know what I'm gonna do . . .

ED

Don't worry. I'll do something.

CUT TO:

EXT. MOVIE STUDIO GATE – MORNING

Ed stands outside MGM, talking into a phone at the guard gate.

ED
(*on phone*)
Mr Feldman! I haven't been able to get through, so I just showed
up. Yeah, out front! So, are we gonna be working together?
(*his face slowly falls*)
Really? Worst film you ever saw . . .?
(*beat*)
Well, my next one will be better.
(*beat*)
Hello?

INT. ED AND DOLORES'S HOUSE – DAY

Dolores tries to cheer up gloomy Ed. He's wearing angora.

ED
I'm no good.

DOLORES
Ed, it's just one man's opinion!

ED
Bela needs a job . . . I can't even get a film going . . .
(*listless*)
But *of course* I can't – I made the worst movie of all time.

DOLORES
That's ridiculous.

Ed sighs.

ED
All I wanna do is tell stories. The things I find interesting . . .

DOLORES
Well, maybe you're not studio kind of material. Maybe you just
need to raise the money yourself.

Ed looks up.

*INT. BANK – DAY

Ed sits opposite a LOAN OFFICER.

* In the completed film these scenes were done with Ed pitching the plea on the telephone.

ED

The movie is called *Bride of the Atom* . . .

INT. DENTIST'S OFFICE — DAY

Ed continues, pitching to three DENTISTS *in white coats.*

ED

. . . It will star Bela Lugosi. Each of you would put up $20,000 . . .

EXT. PHONE BOOTH — DAY

Ed stands at a busy intersection. He yells into a phone.

ED

Yes, that's right. *The* Bela Lugosi. He's still alive.
(*beat*)
Huh? Is he available Friday night? Gee, I suppose so . . . Why?

CUT TO:

INT. TV STUDIO — NIGHT

We're backstage at a 1950s variety show. It's exciting live TV: showgirls, techies and cast members dart about in a state of hyped-up tumult.

*INT. DRESSING ROOM — SAME TIME

Bela and Ed sit in his dressing room, running lines. Bela is in his Count outfit: cape, jet-black hair, red lips, etc. They both read off scripts.

BELA

'Greetings. I am the Count.'

ED

'Greetings. I am Slick Slomopavitz, Seeker of Adventure.'
Audience laughs. Applause. 'Say, that's a funny place to sleep.'

BELA

'It is my home.'

---

* In the completed film Ed and Bela are in the wings backstage.

ED

'Oh, tract housing, huh?' Laugh. 'You need a new real-estate agent.'

BELA

'Beg to differ. This casket incarpratates, er, inporporates –

Ed interrupts.

ED

No Bela, that's 'incorporates.' Look, just say 'This casket has . . .'

BELA
(*upset*)

Ach! How do they expect a Hungarian to pronounce this dialogue? This live television is madness!

An ASSISTANT knocks and sticks her head in.

ASSISTANT

Five minutes, Mr Lugosi.

INT. BACKSTAGE – MINUTES LATER

Ed and Bela stand in the wings. Onstage is the SHOW HOST, a cheesy comedian. He is doing a routine with Criswell, the famed psychic who opened this movie. Criswell wears a tux and a turban and is acting mysteriously.

CRISWELL

*[By 1960, I predict the automobile will have retractable wings, so it can fly.

HOST

Sounds like a heck of a way to beat traffic.

Audience laughs. Criswell rubs his temples enigmatically.]

CRISWELL

By April 19, 1970, I predict Man will have colonized Mars. Millions of people will live there.

Ed is mesmerized.

* Cut from completed film.

61

ED

Wow! Ain't that something.

INT. STUDIO – LATER

We're out in the audience. The curtain rises on a spooky set: shadows, cobwebs and a coffin in the center. The Host walks onstage, to huge applause. He's playing his 'Slick' character, a befuddled moron in a funny hat. The Host shines a flashlight around and then the coffin opens. Bela sits up.

There's more applause.

BELA

Greetings. I am the Count.

HOST

Greetings. I am Slick Slomopavitz, Seeker of Adventure.

The audience laughs. Then applause.

HOST

Say, that's a funny place to sleep.

BELA

It is my home.

HOST

Oh, tract housing, huh?
(*he starts ad-libbing*)
I guess I shouldn't complain about my duplex in Burbank. What a dump. Some places have a Murphy bed, this place has a Murphy *shower*. I still don't know where to hang the towels!

The audience howls with laughter. Bela is totally lost. He seems incredibly confused.

BELA

Uh, beg to differ.

HOST

'Beg to differ'?! Hey bloodsucker, I'm talkin' about my towels!

BELA
(*terrified, groping*)

Uh, Greetings. I am the Count . . .

BACKSTAGE:

Ed covers his face in embarrassment.

CUT TO:

INT. STUDIO HALLWAY – LATER

The Host angrily storms past.

HOST
I told you we should've gotten Karloff.

He exits. A door opens, and Ed and Bela quietly step out.

ED
Bela, don't worry. You're better than all this crap.

BELA
(*distraught*)
I never said I could ad-lib . . .

ED
Forget about it. We'll make our new movie, and you'll be a star
again.

They shuffle away . . . until Criswell and his snazzy ENTOURAGE *burst
around a corner. Even in person, Criswell is ethereal and quite self-
important. He is delighted to see Bela.*

CRISWELL
Mr *Lugosi*! It is an unparalleled privilege to meet you. Allow me to
introduce myself . . . I am *Criswell*!

BELA
(*morose*)
It's a pleasure . . .

CRISWELL
Ah cheer up! Don't lose heart over what happened tonight.
(*he points at his temple*)

I predict that your next project will be an outstanding success!

                         ED

Wow.

                    CRISWELL

And who may you be?

                         ED

Edward Wood, sir.

                    CRISWELL

Ah. The director of *Glen or Glenda*.

                         ED
                     (*statled*)

H-how'd you know?!

                    CRISWELL

I'm Criswell. I know all.

Criswell winks.

CUT TO:

INT. MOCAMBO ROOM – NIGHT

Latin horns blast onstage of this hopping 1950s nightclub. Cigarette girls roam about. Seated at a front table is Ed, Bela and Criswell's group. Everyone's plastered and laughing. Criswell shouts above this din at a WAITER.

                    CRISWELL

Bring me two more Beefeater martinis. Eddie will have another whiskey, Dagmar's a rum and Coke, Moustapha and King are Chablis – hey Bela, would you like a wine?

                      BELA

No. I never drink – wine.

The whole table cracks up. Bela cheers up. Ed turns to Criswell.

                         ED

Hey Cris, how'd you know we'd be living on Mars by 1970? How'd you know it wouldn't be 1975, or even 1980?

                         64

                    CRISWELL
I guessed.

                          ED
I don't understand.

                    CRISWELL
I made it up. It's horseshit!

Ed's jaw drops.

There's no such thing as a psychic. People believe my folderol
because I wear a turban and a black tuxedo.

                          ED
It's that easy?

                    CRISWELL
Eddie, we're in showbiz! It's all about razzle-dazzle.
Appearances. If you dress nice and talk well, people will swallow
anything.

Criswell smiles knowingly. Ed nods at this profound wisdom.

CUT TO:

*[EXT. BROWN DERBY – NIGHT

*We're outside the legendary hat-shaped restaurant. A large Eldorado
pulls up, and a* CONSERVATIVE MAN *and his* PLUMP WIFE *step out and
approach the* DOORMAN

               CONSERVATIVE MAN
Excuse me. We're here for the Wood party.

                    DOORMAN
Ah, that would be in the Venetian Room, sir.

The couple raise their eyebrows. They're impressed.]

* Cut from completed film.

INT. BROWN DERBY – NIGHT

*A large banner says '"*BRIDE OF THE ATOM*" – THIS YEAR'S SMASH HIT!'*

In a private back room, Ed is throwing a lavish backers' party. All his riff-raff friends are dressed in tuxedos and gowns, strutting about with flutes of champagne like they're extras in The Great Gatsby.

Bewildered POTENTIAL BACKERS *wander around. Ed shmoozes them.*

> ED
> We're gonna have the most terrifying monster ever seen on film! A ghastly creature – created from an atomic mutation!

> BACKER'S WIFE
> I don't like scary movies. I go more for ones with love stories.

> ED
> (*without dropping a beat*)
> Well that's what this movie *is* . . . a heartbreaking romance! It's about a young reporter, Janet Lawton, in love with a young cop, Dick Craig.

*[ACROSS THE ROOM:

Conrad and Paul sit in a corner. Conrad has a shoe off and is scratching his foot. Ed alarmedly runs over.

> ED
> What do you think you're doin'?!

> CONRAD
> These shoes are itchy.

> ED
> You *can't sit*! You gotta walk around, with good posture. You want these people to think we have class. Otherwise they'll *never* invest in our movie.]

ACROSS THE PARTY:

Two AMAZED BACKERS *have their hands around Tor's giant arm.*

* Cut from completed film.

66

AMAZED BACKER
Bernie, get a load of this guy!

                    TOR
              (*proud of his size*)
Biceps twenty-two! Chest sixty-two! Stomach fifty-four!

                AMAZED BACKER
Whew! You're quite a specimen.
                  (*beat*)
And you're gonna be in the picture?

                    TOR
Yes. I play Lobo!

*[ACROSS THE ROOM:

An excited HICK BACKER *shakes Bela's hand.*

                HICK BACKER
Mr Lugosi, I can't believe I'm meeting you in person. This is one
of the most exciting moments of my life.

                    BELA
Thank you. And you are?

                HICK BACKER
Charlie Johnson! I manufacture toothpaste tubes.]

ACROSS THE PARTY:

Criswell struts in the background, talking to someone.

                  CRISWELL
I predict *Bride of the Atom* will be the biggest moneymaker of all
time!

In the foreground, Ed introduces Dolores to a SOUTHERN BACKER.

                    ED
And this is lovely starlet Dolores Fuller, who will play Janet
Lawton.

* Cut from completed film.

> SOUTHERN BACKER

And how much will this picture cost?

> ED

In a normal studio – it would be half a million, with all their wasteful overheads and fancy offices. But because we're more efficient, we can bring it in for seventy grand!

> SOUTHERN BACKER

Hmm. Well, I'll consider it . . .

EXT. BROWN DERBY – LATER THAT NIGHT

Ed and his buddies wave goodbye to the departing backers.

> ED

Goodbye! Goodbye!

> BELA
> (*to Ed*)

So how'd we do?

> ED
> (*faking a big smile, but* sotto voce *to Bela*)

We didn't make a dime.

*[IN THE PARKING LOT:

A VALET *hands the car keys to the Conservative backer.*

> VALET

That's twenty-five cents, sir.

The man glances at his wife. She shrugs.

> WIFE

I gave all my money to the babysitter.

The man grimaces. He checks his pockets, pulls out a handful of pennies and counts them out . . .

CUT TO:

* Cut from completed film.

68

EXT. ED AND DOLORES'S BACKYARD – DAY

Ed sits in a chaise longe by the pool, studying papers and drinking shots of whiskey. He's in a woman's pantsuit and fuzzy slippers. Dolores marches out.

>   DOLORES
> Ed, the landlord called again. He wants his money.

>   ED
> Tell him *Bride* is in pre-production.

>   DOLORES
> Ed, the landlord doesn't care.

>   ED
> That's the problem! *Nobody* cares about my movie! I'm tryin' so hard, I don't know what else to do!

>   DOLORES
> Don't get angry at me. Maybe you just need a day job.

>   ED
>   (*upset*)
> Dolores, don't you understand? I'm a director now! I made *Glen or Glenda*. Directing *is* my day job.

>   DOLORES
>   (*irate*)
> All I know is, ever since *Glen or Glenda*, all you do is booze it up and wear my clothes!

Suddenly Paul hesitantly steps through the back gate.

>   PAUL MARCO
> Uh, yoo-hoo. Excuse me! Sorry to interrupt, but I got some big news.

>   ED
>   (*dour*)
> Yeah . . . ?

>   PAUL MARCO
> Well – my cousin Fred met this dame from back East. She's from 'old money', and he thinks she's loaded. And here's the kicker:

69

she's *very interested* in the picture business!

ANGLE – ED:

He slowly smiles. It's like sun breaking through rain clouds.

CUT TO:]

*EXT. RESTAURANT PATIO – DAY

We're at a fancy outdoor brunch. Ed is shaking hands with pretty
LORETTA KING, *twenty-five, a pale brunette in a classy dress.*

LORETTA

Pleased to meet you. I'm Loretta King.

ED

I understand you just moved here?

LORETTA

Yes. Hollywood is, oh, so exciting.

A WAITER *walks over, with a water pitcher.*

WAITER

Water, ma'am?

LORETTA
(*suddenly freaking out*)

No! No water! *No liquids!* I'm terribly allergic to them!

The waiter is bewildered. He hurries away. Ed leans in.

ED

So my associate Mr Marco tells me you may be interested in
investing in a motion picture.

LORETTA

Perhaps a small amount of money.
(*she smiles*)
How much do one of your motion pictures cost?

ED

For this one, we need $60,000.

---

* In the completed film Ed meets Loretta by chance in a bar.

LORETTA

That's all?? That seems very reasonable for an entire picture.

Ed perks up. She's a live one!

Ed pulls a script from his briefcase and hands it to her.

ED

Perhaps you'd like to look at the photoplay.

LORETTA

Oh my, this is very interesting.
(*she skims the pages*)
Say . . . do you think it would be possible for me to play one of these parts?

ED
(*very enthused*)
Oh, of course!! There's a couple characters you'd be perfect for: the secretary at the newspaper office, or the file clerk!

LORETTA

Hmm. Those sound kind of small.
(*stopping at a page*)
Oh, here's one that looks good: Janet Lawton. I'd sure like to play her.

Ed blanches.

ED

J-Janet Lawton???

LORETTA

Yes, Janet Lawton is clearly the part to play. She's got some real meaty scenes! Can't you just see *me* in that part??

CU – ED:

He is aghast. What a stomach-churning decision. He stares at Loretta, then slow croaks a response.

ED

Uh . . . yeah . . .
(*beat*)
You'd be perfect.

CUT TO:

EXT. ED AND DOLORES'S HOUSE – DAY

We hear dishes being violently thrown. Dolores screams inside.

> DOLORES
> (*off*)
> You bastard! You two-timing, dress-wearing son-of-a-*bitch*!!

INT. HOUSE – SAME TIME

Dolores is crying and screaming angrily. Ed ducks the objects she hurls at him.

> ED
> It was the only way I could get the movie made!

> DOLORES
> Who do you think's been paying the rent?! Who helped type your script, and did all your grunt work?!

> ED
> I'm sorry! What did you want me to say?

> DOLORES
> I wanted you to say, 'No! I wrote the part for my girlfriend Dolores.'

> ED
> But there's plenty of other parts.

> DOLORES
> Like *what*?!

> ED
> (*nervous*)
> The secretary. Or the file clerk.

Dolores is stunned.

> DOLORES
> *You asshole!*

She hurls a pot at Ed. Whack! It slams him in the head.

CUT TO:

INT. SOUNDSTAGE – DAY

The sets are being erected for Bride of the Atom. *The* CREW *hurries about the small stage, as Ed energetically supervises. He has a large Band-Aid on his head.**

> ED
>
> This is gonna be Bela's laboratory, so it should be real impressive! Like one of those mad-scientist movies. I want beakers, and test tubes, and one of those electrical things that buzzes!

> PAUL MARCO
>
> You mean a Tesla coil?

> ED
>
> If you say so.

†[*Tor lumbers over, in his ripped Lobo outfit. His face has fake gashed-up scars. Tor holds the script.*

> TOR
>
> Edvard! I haf question 'bout script. My wife Greta, she read. And she no like.

> ED
>
> Really? Was the third act too intense?

> TOR
> (*trying to be polite*)
> No. She tink Lobo is waste of my time. Lobo don't talk.

> ED
>
> But Tor, it's a starring part! You're second billed.

> TOR
>
> Bela, he talk. Loretta, she talk. But Tor, he no talk.

Ed thinks. He quickly puts a spin on this.

---

* In the completed film Ed is clutching an ice bag to the back of his head.
† Cut from completed film.

                              ED

Tor, dialogue is overrated. You look at the classic film actors, who
are they? Fairbanks. Chaplin. They didn't talk! They did it all with
their face.

                             TOR
                        (*still bothered*)
But Greta say –]

Loretta walks over, holding two dresses.

                           LORETTA
Eddie, which dress do you like better?

                              ED
I don't know.
                         (*he yells off*)
Hey Bill, which dress is better for you, the green or the red one?

Cameraman Bill is standing at the camera. He squints.

                       CAMERAMAN BILL
Which one *is* the red one?

                              ED
                         (*confused*)
What do you mean?

                       CAMERAMAN BILL
I mean I can't see the difference. I'm color-blind.
                            (*beat*)
But I like the dark gray one.

WIPE TO:

INT. SOUNDSTAGE – LATER

The crew is shooting on a spooky castle foyer set.

                              ED
Action!

*Bela enters, wearing a lab-coat costume. As he slowly crosses, the old man
rubs his hands fiendishly. Ed yells live direction through a megaphone.*

                              74

Okay, you're Dr Eric Vornoff. You're upset. You've worked so hard on this experiment and you don't want to see it fail.

Bela stops, to 'emote'.

No, you're not *that* upset. You want to keep moving. You wanna cross the room.

Bela exits.

Okay, *cut! Beautiful! Print it!*
            (Ed claps his hands triumphantly.)
Alright, let's go immediately to scene fifty-two. Tor, are you in place?

TOR'S VOICE

Yah.

ED

Okay, *cue rainstorm!*

Behind the window, Conrad pours a watering can.

And roll camera! *Action!*

Tor enters, but can barely squeeze his bulk through the door. Finally he enters. Ed yells through the megaphone.

Okay, you're Lobo. You're upset. You've worked so hard helping Dr Vornoff on this experiment, and you don't want to see it fail.

Tor stops, to 'emote'.

No, you're not *that* upset. You want to keep moving. You wanna cross the room.

Tor exits. The set shakes as he has trouble getting through the door.

Okay, *cut! Perfect! Print it!*

*[OFFSTAGE:

Bela talks to Tor.

---

* In the completed film this sequence comes at the beginning of the scene.

BELA
At Universal, they shot two scenes a day. Eddie can knock off
twenty or thirty! He's incredible.]

BACK ON SET:

Cameraman Bill leans in to Ed.

CAMERAMAN BILL
Hey Ed, shouldn't we do another take? Big Baldy kinda got stuck
in the doorway.

ED
No, it's fine. It's real! In actuality, Lobo would struggle with that
problem every day.

WIPE TO:

INT. LABORATORY SET – LATER

*[They are back on the completed lab set. Beyond the Bunsen burners and
beakers is a kitchenette in the corner.*

ED
Wow, this lab looks great. Except – why is there a stove and
refrigerator?

PAUL MARCO
We couldn't afford any more props. If it seems weird, maybe you
can add a scene where they eat dinner.

ED
Nah, it'll work. Where's Bela?

OFFSTAGE:

Bela is asleep on a couch. Ed nudges him.

ED
Bela, are you ready?

BELA
(*he groggily wakes up*)
Hrmph? Where am I?

* Cut from completed film.

76

ED

You're shooting *Bride of the Atom*. Scene eighty-five.

Bela nods. He stands up, then grimaces in pain. So he pulls two bright little pills from his pocket and swallows them.]

Ed walks Bela onto the lab set.

ED

You'll be sitting on the right.

BELA
(*he glares at the sparkling Tesla coils*)
I'm not getting near that goddamn thing. One of those burned me on *The Return of Chandu*.

ED

Okay. Then you'll be sitting on the *left*.

Ed turns to Tor and Loretta. She wears a wedding gown.

Here's the scene. Loretta, you're in a trance. You glide in and get on the operating table. Now Tor, you're supposed to tie her down. But you have an angora fetish . . . and when you rub the swatch of angora, it makes you refuse – so Bela has to discipline you.

TOR

Okey-dokey.

WIPE TO:

INT. SHOOTING – LATER

The scene begins.

ED

Action!

BELA (*as* VORNOFF)
'Now we are ready for the girl.'

Bela does his patented hypnotic arm move. He actually has a powerful intensity. Loretta staggers in, eyes glazed. Like a zombie, she climbs onto the operating table.

*['Dear, you are a woman of super strength and beauty. A lovely vision of exquisitely beauty' – shit!
>(*he breaks character*)

Damn! Eddie, I'm sorry – I can't remember all this. I'm an old man. It's too long.

ED

That's fine, Bela. We're still rolling. Just say, 'Dear, you're lovely.'

BELA
>(*he snaps back into character*)

'Dear, you're lovely.'
>(*he turns to Tor*)

'Strap her to the table.']

Tor starts to tie Loretta down, then gets distracted by a piece of angora hooked to his waist. He rubs it lovingly, calmed, then suddenly refuses.

Bela is furious.

BELA (*as* VORNOFF)

'Do as I command you!'

Bela pulls out an oversized bullwhip and starts whipping Tor. Tor screams in agony.

BELA (*as* VORNOFF)

'I'll teach you to disobey me!'

Bela chases Tor around the set, whipping him.

ED

*[And, *cut*!!! Impeccable!

ON TOR:

He dances about happily.

TOR

I love being movie star!

Tor jubilantly hugs Loretta. She grimaces.

---

* Cut from completed film.

LORETTA

Ow. Not so hard, Tor.]

ON ED:

A SURLY STAGE MANAGER *strides over to Ed.*

SURLY STAGE MANAGER

Hey, Wood. Your check bounced.

ED

Okay, I'll get you the money later.

SURLY STAGE MANAGER

No. I need it *now*.

Ed nods grimly. He grabs Loretta and takes her aside.

ED

Sorry to bother you while we're shooting, but the guy who owns the stage needs his money.

LORETTA

Well then you should pay him, shouldn't you?

ED
(he smiles)

Yeah. Exactly!

There's a pause. They stare at each other.

I kinda need it now.

LORETTA
(baffled)

What are you looking at me like that for? I already gave you my three hundred.

ED

Yeah. Well, I need the other sixty thousand.

LORETTA

What other sixty thousand?

ED

The other sixty thousand you said you'd give me.

> LORETTA

You misunderstood. I gave you everything I have in the world: three hundred dollars.

CU – ED:

He looks like he's going to throw up.

> ED

Oh my God.

CUT TO:

EXT. SOUNDSTAGE – DAY

The large stage door slams shut.

Ed's disoriented cast and crew stand in the street. Bela, Tor and Loretta are still in costume.

Ed looks totally dazed. He blinks in the bright sunlight.

CUT TO:

INT. BROWN DERBY – NIGHT

We're back at the Brown Derby, for another backers' party. The same banner is hanging: '"BRIDE OF THE ATOM" – THIS YEAR'S SMASH HIT!'

The whole crowd is there (except Dolores), dressed up. Bela sits in the corner, knocking back a drink.

> BELA

Here we go again.

Ed stands with a circle of POTENTIAL BACKERS. He has an edge of desperation we've never seen before.

> ED

. . . lemme tell you, you can't lose. It's scary! And if you don't like that, it's romantic! Bela Lugosi portrays Dr Vornoff, and lovely ingenue Loretta King is reporter Janet Lawton.

Hmm. Lugosi looks pretty old.
>   (*he squints across the room*)
Which role is Vampira playing?

ED

Vampira . . . ?
>   (*bewildered*)
Why do you ask??

POTENTIAL BACKER

Well, I see her standing over there.

The guy points. Ed turns and looks – and Vampira is standing in the next room. She's at a different party.

ED

Well . . . she's playing –
>   (*beat*)
Could you excuse me one moment??

Ed dashes from the room.

NEXT ROOM OVER:

Vampira is drinking with a bunch of artsy-fartsy types. She's in street clothes, but clearly recognizable. Ed runs up.

ED

Excuse me, Miss Vampira?

VAMPIRA

Yes?

ED
>   (*sweaty*)
You don't know me, but my name is Ed Wood. I'm a film producer. I'm currently in production on a science-fiction piece, with Bela Lugosi and Swedish wrestler Tor Johnson. And I saw you here, and I thought: Kismet!

Vampira stares, totally uncomprehending.

VAMPIRA

I don't understand. Do you want my autograph?

81

ED
No. I think my film is perfect for you.

VAMPIRA
You want me to show it on my TV program? Well, I got nothing to
do with that. You should call up the station manager at Channel 7 –

ED
(*unyielding*)
No! I don't want you to show the movie, I want you to be *in it*!
See, maybe I should explain: we started shooting, but then after
three days we got shut down. So we're having a backers' party, to
raise some more money. Perhaps you'd like to come next door and
meet some of the backers . . . ?

Vampira glances at her friends. They uncomfortably turn away.

VAMPIRA
Uh, look, I'm with some friends, and we're about to eat –

ED
(*begging*)
Please! It'll only take a minute. You can have some hors-
d'oeuvres, and meet my backers! There's a really nice dentist from
Oxnard . . .

VAMPIRA
(*pissed of*)
Look buddy, I'm a big star. I've got real offers from real studios.
I don't need to blow some dentist for a part. So forget it!

BACK AT THE PARTY:

*The backers glance into the next room. Ed is in front of Vampira, begging
on his hands and knees.*

BACKER
(*to another backer*)
I'm getting a bad feeling about this. Let's get out of here.

*[The backers pick up their coats. Through the doorway, Ed sees this. He
jumps up and frantically runs back in.*

* Cut from completed film.

ED
Where are you guys going? You can't leave!

BACKER
(*running out*)
Goodbye, Mr Wood.

ED
(*insane*)
You can't go! You haven't seen the storyboards!

The backers run out of the room. They're gone.

Ed shouts after them.

Fine! *Screw you!* If you don't have the balls to roll the dice, then I don't want your stinking money!!

No response.

Please, come back!

CUT TO:

EXT. ED AND DOLORES'S HOUSE – DAY

Ed and Dolores are being evicted. Their belongings are scattered in front. They bitterly carry furniture out of the house. Ed stumbles and slurs his speech. He is drunk.

ED
Goddamn landlord.

DOLORES
I told you this was gonna happen.

ED
Maybe if you'd come to the backers party, I would've gotten the money.

DOLORES
That's moronic. Why would a bit player impress a backer?

ED
(*he starts yelling*)
Look, how many times can I say I'm sorry? I blew it! I thought
she was rich.

DOLORES
That's a good reason to dump your girlfriend?

ED
I didn't dump you! Get it through your skull – I just recast the part!

Ed drops the furniture. He flops onto the sidewalk.

DOLORES
You're a fuckin' mess.

ED
So *what*? Look, we gotta figure out where we're gonna stay.

DOLORES
I'm going to my mother's.

ED
Does she have room for me?

Dolores shakes her head.

DOLORES
I think you should stay with one of your friends.

CUT TO:

EXT. TOWERING TEMPLE – NIGHT

*Ed and Bela stroll through a parking lot. Ed is sobered up and
remorseful. Bela wears a beret and smokes a huge cigar.*

ED
Bela, I don't know what I'm doin' anymore . . .

BELA
Stop worrying. This is going to raise your spirits.

*They reach the strange entrance to an avant-garde, Eastern-based, quasi-
religious temple. Bela puts out his cigar and they enter the oversized doors.*

84

I CRISWELL: Can your hearts stand the shocking facts of the true story of Edward D. Wood, Junior?

2 BELA: Vampira! You will come under my spell!

3   VAMPIRA

4   *Glen or Glenda*

5   ED: Well, Mr Feldman, some people have resumés to show. I've
got my own movie.

6   ED: My God, look at that guy. He's a mountain!

7   ED: We didn't make a dime.

8   The shooting of *Bride of the Atom* . . .

9   . . . and the première.

10   BELA: So, Eddie, what is the scene about?

11   ED: You're the ruler of the galaxy! Show a little *taste*!

12　Tor rises from the grave . . .

13　. . . and joins Vampira walking in a trance through the cemetery.

14 BUNNY: What plan will we follow?
ALIEN: Plan 9.

15 ED: And *cut! Print it! It's a wrap!*

INT. TEMPLE — SAME TIME

Sphinxes and Bodhisattvas peer down from the marble walls. A service is in progress. A wiry, enigmatic LECTURER *speaks.*

LECTURER

Thou eternal sun, who has covered the consciousness with thy golden disc, do thou remove the veil so that I may see the truth within?

Bela leads Ed to a seat, stepping past men in fezzes and odd elderly women in fur coats. As the lecture continues, Ed whispers in bafflement.

ED

What is this place?

BELA

This is the Philosophical Research Society. A refuge for free thinkers. I've been coming here for twenty years.

LECTURER

. . . for the truth which is within thee is within me. And I am Truth.

BELA

Most people in this country, they know nothing about Eastern mysticism. They are afraid of it.

(*beat*)

But I am open-minded. It gives me hope.

LECTURER

We have the wisdom to govern and the divine right to inherit the earth in good condition. We have the power to build worlds.

Ed leans in to Bela.

ED

Was I wrong to cast Loretta?

BELA

Bad decisions are easy to live with. Forget. Just keep looking forward.

ED

But was it a bad decision? At the time, I thought her money would save the movie.

BELA

Eddie, you screwed up.

ED
(*he nods*)

Yeah, I did.

CUT TO:

INT. TEMPLE — LATER

The lecture is over. The speaker shakes hands with people. Bela leads Ed along.

BELA

In life, the decisions that haunt you are the ones where you just don't know . . . where right or wrong will never be answered.
(*beat*)
Years ago, the Hungarians contacted me. The government wanted me to come home, to be Minister of Culture.

ED

Really?

BELA

It was a very impressive offer. Fancy offices, a big home . . . I'd be treated like a king.

ED

So why didn't you do it?

BELA

I didn't know if it was a trick. They might arrest me and throw me in a gulag.
(*pause*)
I am Hungary's most famous emigrant. They'd use me as a lesson to anyone who tried to leave.

ED

But maybe not.

BELA

Correct. So instead, I stayed here, waiting for my comeback.

86

Always hoping . . . the next film, the next film . . . that would be the one.

They reach the exit. Ed stops in the huge doorway.

ED
Your next film. That *will* be the one.

Bela smiles sweetly.]

CUT TO:

INT. MCCOY MEAT-PACKING PLANT – DAY

We're in a noisy meat-packing plant. WORKERS *in blood-stained aprons slam cleavers into hunks of beef.*

Ed walks down an aisle with DONALD E. MCCOY, *a wealthy Texan meat man. Old Man McCoy is a tough-talking, tobacco-chewing straight-shooter.*

ED
. . . and then Dr Vornoff falls in the pit, and his own octopus attacks and eats him! The End.

OLD MAN MCCOY
Whew! That's quite a story. So you made the movie, and now you want to make it again?

ED
(*gently correcting him*)
No. We shot ten minutes of the movie, and now we're looking for completion funds.

OLD MAN MCCOY
Son, you're too vague. I come from the world of business. I need to know what I get for my investment.

*[ED
Movies are very popular. You could make a lot of money.

OLD MAN MCCOY
Yeah, but most of 'em flop, don't they? What am I tangibly guaranteed?

* Cut from completed film.

87

ED

Well . . . you get 'Executive Producer' credit.

OLD MAN MCCOY

That don't mean diddley.]
                    (*he suddenly shouts angrily*)
Billy Bob! You're cutting 'em *too lean.*

McCoy grabs a cleaver from a worker and slams it into a chop.

ED

Mr McCoy, how can I make you happy?

OLD MAN MCCOY

Cut to the chase, heh? That's good! That's very good.
                    (*McCoy spits his tobacco.*)
Okay, two things. Number one: I want the movie to end with a
big explosion. Sky full of smoke.

ED

But the story ends with Dr Vornoff falling in the pit –

OLD MAN MCCOY

Not anymore. And number two: I've got a son. He's a little slow –
but a good boy. And something tells me he'd make a hell of a
leading man . . .

Under Ed's cheery frozen smile, his face clearly falls.

CUT TO:

*[INT. SALT LAKE CITY AUDITORIUM – NIGHT

*We're at a rowdy wrestling match. Tor Johnson is in the middle of a
screaming, four-man tag-team event. Tor throws his opponent to the
ground, then tags with his partner and goes to the corner.*

Suddenly a WRESTLING COACH *runs up, dragging a telephone on a very
long cord.*

WRESTLING COACH

Tor, you got a phone call!

*Cut from completed film.

TOR

Heh? *Now?*

WRESTLING COACH

They said it was an emergency!

He hands sweaty Tor the phone. Tor speaks into it.

TOR

Hallo?

ED'S VOICE

Tor, this is Ed! Glad I could find you! I got the money and we resume shooting tomorrow morning!

TOR

But I'm in Utah.

ED'S VOICE

Then you'll have to drive all night! I'm counting on you, big guy. Breakfast is at seven.

Click. Ed hangs up. Tor is flabbergasted.

CUT TO:]

INT. SOUNDSTAGE — EARLY MORNING

Bride of the Atom is back in production! Ed's stock company is reunited. People drink coffee and gossip.

PAUL MARCO

This is unbelievable! I woulda bet a million bucks that Ed wouldn't finish this picture.

CAMERAMAN BILL

It ain't finished yet. Anything could happen.

The stage door opens – and standing there, in silhouette, is Dolores. Everybody goes quiet. People glance nervously at Loretta.

Uh-oh. Stay out of scratching distance.

89

AT DOLORES:

Ed runs over. Dolores is beautifully made-up and wearing a furry angora sweater. Ed speaks, awkwardly.

> ED
>
> Honey, you made it! I wasn't sure you got my message.

> DOLORES
> *(icy)*
>
> Of course I'm here. Today is the file clerk's big scene.

> ED
>
> That's right . . .

> DOLORES
>
> I see the usual gang of misfits and dope addicts are here.
> *(she looks around)*
> Say, who's the lug?

In a corner, standing by himself, is dumb TONY MCCOY, *Old Man McCoy's worthless son. He's a good-looking, moody hunk. Tony is practising his lines from a script, but he's terribly stiff.*

> TONY
>
> 'Now Janet, I want you straying away – oops – *staying* away from the Old Willows place.'

Ed shrugs.

> ED
>
> That's Tony McCoy. He's playing Lieutenant Dick Craig.

> DOLORES
>
> Oh really? How much money did he put up?

> ED
>
> None.
> *(beat)*
> But his dad gave me fifty grand.

> DOLORES
> *(snide)*
>
> Wood Productions. The mark of quality.

ED

Hey, *the movie's getting made.* That's the main thing.

Dolores shakes her head contemptuously. Then she strides off. Ed stands alone, feeling bad.

WIPE TO:

ON STAGE:

The set is a one-wall 'office hallway': a doorway and a water cooler. Loretta sits in a make-up chair, as Harry works on her.

DOLORES
(*off*)

Hey, Harry – long time no see.

Harry turns, surprised. Dolores stands behind him. There's a thick tension. He smiles anxiously.

MAKE-UP MAN HARRY

Hi, Dolores . . .

LORETTA

Oh, you're Dolores?! I've heard so much about you! I'm Loretta King.
(*she chipperly jumps up*)
Here, take the chair.

DOLORES
(*bitchy*)

Don't be silly – let Harry finish. You still need more work.

LORETTA

No, I'm done. All I needed was a touch-up.

DOLORES

Mm, that mole still shows.

Loretta frowns. Ed quickly steps in.

ED

Ladies! You both look fine. Why don't we talk about the scene?
(*beat*)
Okay. Janet Lawton has discovered that Dr Vornoff bought the

Old Willows estate. So now she wants to prove that all the monster stories are true.

Dolores nods sourly. She's in a trouble-making mood.

> DOLORES
>
> Eddie, what's *my* motivation?

> ED
> *(thrown off)*
>
> Oh. Er . . . well you're the file clerk. You're hurrying into the next room, when you bump into Janet.

> DOLORES
>
> But what's our relationship? Are we good friends, or is she just a casual acquaintance?

> ED
> *(annoyed)*
>
> Dolores, I got five days to shoot this movie. Don't get goofy on me.

WIPE TO:

*INT. SCREENING ROOM – NIGHT

We're watching dailies.

ON SCREEN:

A camera assistant claps the slate. We hear Ed yell: 'Action!'

Loretta hurries down the hallway. Dolores sees her run past and shouts out.

> DOLORES (*as* FILE CLERK)
>
> 'Janet, the boss has been looking for you.'

> LORETTA (*as* JANET LAWTON)
>
> 'Thanks.'

Loretta runs out. Dolores just stands there. We hear Ed: 'Cut! Perfect!'

Dolores turns deadpan to the camera.

> DOLORES
>
> Of course it was.

* In the completed film this scene actually takes place on the set.

The film runs out.

ON THE AUDIENCE:

The screening-room lights come up on the crew. Ed sits in a gloomy haze.

Suddenly, there's loud clapping from the back of the room.

> CRISWELL
> Bravo! Bravo! Magnifico!

> ED
> (*he smiles*)
> Cris, you made it. Thanks a lot.

> CRISWELL
> My pleasure. I'm always happy to assist in a little larceny.

CUT TO:

*[EXT. STREET – NIGHT

Criswell's long pink Cadillac convertible races down the street. Ed and Criswell are in front, and Tor, Conrad and Paul are stuffed into the back.

> TOR
> My head is cold.

> CRISWELL
> You know how much this car cost me?

> CONRAD
> Two thousand dollars.

> CRISWELL
> Wrong! *One dollar!* Miss Mae West herself sold it to me. She said, 'Cris, you belong in a pink Cadillac!'

Conrad frowns. Criswell turns to Ed.

> CRISWELL
> Incidentally, you *promise* you're not going to scratch my car . . .?

---

* Cut from completed film.

ED
(*cocky*)
I told you, the octopus is made of rubber. This is a piece o' cake.

EXT. REPUBLIC STUDIOS – NIGHT

Ed and the guys climb over a fence. They're breaking into Republic Studios. Paul is panicked.

PAUL MARCO
Ed! You said you were getting permission.

ED
Eh, I couldn't reach the guy . . . he was in meetings all day. But this'll be fine. I promise!

Paul glances at Conrad. Conrad shrugs. Tor struggles to get over, but is too massive.

TOR
I'm no good at climbink.

Tor gives up, and simply bashes through the locked gate. Everyone is amazed. Tor laughs.

I'm good at bashink!!

CRISWELL
Hey, keep it down. My publicist will throttle me if we get caught.

They all sneak across the shadowy lot. Remnants of old scary sets tower over them.]

OUTSIDE A SOUNDSTAGE:

They reach a stage door. Ed tries it – but it's locked.

ED
Oh. I thought they kept this open.

A pause. Everyone looks at Tor. He grins.

TOR
Lobo will fix!

Tor grabs the heavy door and easily snaps the lock.

INT. SOUNDSTAGE – SAME TIME

This place is the mythic eclectic prop room. Guillotines, rocketships, a stuffed vulture . . . strange mysterious props from untold movies loom everywhere in the darkness.

It's a place of wonderment and fear.

The men stare in awe.

> CONRAD

Wow.

> PAUL MARCO

This place gives me the creeps. Let's get the hell out of here.

> ED

Not so fast. First, we have to get it down.

Ed gestures above. Everyone glances straight up.

THEIR POV:

A giant octopus is lashed to the ceiling.

> CUT TO:

INT. SOUNDSTAGE – LATER

Conrad and Criswell are way up on the catwalk, holding onto dangling Paul by his belt. Paul leans way out, reaching for the octopus. He shouts nervously.

> PAUL MARCO

You're sure this is gonna work?

> ED
> (off)

Yes!

> PAUL MARCO

You're *sure*???

> ED
> (off)

Yes! Just do it!

WIDE VIEW:

Standing straight below is Tor. The Swede has his arms outstretched, waiting.

Ed supervises a good distance away. He motions to Paul.

Paul gulps, then unties the octopus.

It drops incredibly fast. The thing must weigh half a ton.

Tor's eyes widen.

And the octopus smashes straight on top of him.

Bam!

Tor is gone from sight. One of the eight tentacles snaps off.

UP IN THE CATWALK:

Criswell moans.

> CRISWELL
> Oh my God. We killed him.

ON THE GROUND:

Ed runs to the octopus and looks for Tor underneath.

> ED
> Tor! Are you okay?!

A beat. And then the octopus flips over. Tor sits up, battered but smiling.

> TOR
> Bedder than wrestlink!

*[EXT. REPUBLIC STUDIOS – NIGHT

The five men hurry across the lot, carrying the humongous octopus on their shoulders.

Suddenly, a flashlight shines on them.

---

* Cut from completed film.

ANGRY VOICE

Hey! What are you doing?

The men jump with fear. They break into a fast waddling run.

CRISWELL

Thank God Tor broke the fence.

The team runs through the busted gate and escape.

EXT. STUDIOS – NIGHT

The Cadillac screeches away. The octopus flops on top of the five men.

WIPE TO:]

EXT. GRIFFITH PARK – NIGHT

The movie crew is setting up for a big night shoot. Lights and generators are sprawled across this isolated area.

Tony McCoy perches goofily on his own personalized chair. He runs lines by himself.

TONY

'Now Janet, I want you staying away from the Old Willows place.'

The octopus lays in a dried-up riverbed. There's only about an inch of water. Ed yells at Conrad.

ED

You don't understand! The octopus is supposed to live in a *lake*!

CONRAD

This is kind of a stream –

ED

No! It has to be *underwater*!

Ed storms away. Conrad scratches his head.

IN A DUSTY PARKING LOT:

Bela sits inertly in the back of an open car. He weakly hails over Ed.

97

BELA

Eddie, I'm so tired . . . I don't know if I can handle a night shoot . . .

ED

Nonsense! You look great –
    (*suddenly he catches himself; he speaks more sincerely*)
Look, uh, why don't you lie down and take a little nap? We'll film around you for a while.

BELA

Thanks, buddy . . .

Ed smiles warmly, then walks off.

Bela stares after him, then absent-mindedly searches through his pockets. Finally, he finds what he's looking for – a rubber tube. Bela looks to make sure no one's around, then ties the tube around his upper arm . . .

EXT. SET – LATER

Crew members have dammed up the end of the river and Conrad fills it with a hose. There is now a foot of water.

Ed stands at the shore, admiring it.

ED

Hey. This is looking good!
                (*he turns to Paul*)
Paul, where's the octopus motor?

PAUL MARCO

What octopus motor?

ED

You know, to make the legs move –

PAUL MARCO
(*defensive*)
Hey, don't blame me! You didn't say anything about no motor when I was up on that ceiling!

Bela stumbles up, with a dazed smile.

                              BELA
Let's shoot this fucker! Where do I go?

                               ED
You'll be fighting with the octopus.

                              BELA
Out *there*?!
                    (*he points at the water*)
What happened to the stream?

                               ED
This'll look a lot better. We have to match the stock footage of the
octopus underwater.

                              BELA
Oh, for Christ's sake.

Bela wades out, into the water.

  Goddamn, it's cold!

                               ED
Once you're in it, it warms up.

                              BELA
Fuck you! You come out here.
                           (*beat*)
Hey, toss me that JD.

A crew member throws Bela a bottle of Jack Daniels.

*Bela pops the cap and chugs half the bottle in one swig. He licks his lips,
then turns towards the octopus.*

  Okay! How do we turn this thing on?

                               ED
Eh, somebody misplaced the motor. So when you wrestle the
octopus, shake the legs a bit, to make it look like it's killing you.

Bela stares, deadpan.

                              BELA
Do you know I turned down *Frankenstein*?

                               99

ED

Huh?

BELA

After I did *Dracula*, the studio offered me *Frankenstein*! But I turned it down. The part wasn't sexy enough. It was too degrading for a big star like me.

The crew glances at Ed.

ED

Bela, I've got twenty-five scenes to shoot tonight.

BELA

Don't let me slow you down.

ED

Alright! Let's put it on film. *Camera! Sound!*

Bela takes another swig of JD, then throws it offcamera.

Action!

Bela starts flailing around the octopus legs and screaming in horror. This image is truly ridiculous.

Ed is pleased.

Some crew members nod: pretty good.

ED

And *cut!* That was perfect!

Everybody cheers.

*[*Then suddenly the dam walls burst.*

Whoosh! The water rushes from the lake and floods the park below.]

WIPE TO:

EXT. DINKY SOUNDSTAGES – EARLY MORNING

Crew members straggle in for the final shoot. Everybody looks bleary-eyed from last night. Ed stands cheerily at the entrance, greeting them.

* Cut from completed film.

ED

C'mon! Just one more day! Just have some coffee, you'll feel better!

Tony staggers up.

TONY

Mr Wood, I only got one hour of sleep.

ED

Yeah? Well I got *no* sleep, and I feel great!

Ed sees Bela slowly shuffling along. Ed runs over to him.

Bela. I just wanna thank you again for last night.

BELA
(*exhausted*)

That's fine, Eddie. All in the line of duty.

ED

No. Seriously. I want you to know how much I appreciate what you've done for me. A great man like you shouldn't have to run around in freezing water at four in the morning.

BELA

Well, there aren't too many other fellas I'd do it for . . .

Ed smiles, then pulls out a script page.

ED

I wrote something special for you. I got to thinking about all the sacrifices you've made . . . and so I wrote you a new final speech.

Ed hands him the paper. Bela starts reading it, as Ed watches anxiously. Bela is very touched.

BELA
(*still reading*)

Eddie, this is quite a scene.

ED

I know it's a lot to give you at the last second.

Bela looks up.

BELA

These lines – I'll have no problem remembering.

WIPE TO:

INT. SOUNDSTAGE – DAY

They are shooting. Ed watches offcamera as Bela acts a somber scene with an actor playing PROFESSOR STROWSKI, *a threatening European.*

STOWSKI

'Our government wants you to return . . . to continue your experiments there. Where you can have everything at your disposal.'

BELA (*as* VORNOFF)

'My dear Professor Strowski, twenty years ago I was banned from my homeland. I was classed as a madman – a charlatan – outlawed in the world of science which previously honored me as a genius!'
(*he gets very subdued*)
'Now here in this forsaken jungle hell, I have proven that I am alright.'

STOWSKI

'Yes, the authorities have learned how correct your findings were. So I am here – sent to bring you home.'

BELA
(*impassioned*)
'Home. I have no home. Hunted . . . despised . . . living like an animal – the jungle is my home! But I will show the world that I can be its master. I shall perfect my own race of people – a race of atomic supermen that will conquer the world!'

It's an incredible performance of crowning tragedy. Bela is totally drained.

CU – ED:

He is very moved. He whispers, barely audible.

ED

Cut. It's a wrap.

CUT TO:

INT. MEAT-PACKING PLANT – NIGHT

The wrap party is being thrown in the meat-packing plant. People laugh and shout and carry on. Tor pours booze in the punch. R&B music plays. Old Man McCoy dances with Loretta. Bunny dances with a young stud. Dolores stands by herself.

*[Bela and Criswell are giggling.

                    CRISWELL
So *you* sleep in coffins?!

                    BELA
Yes. There is nothing more comfortable.

                    CRISWELL
I can't believe this! *I* sleep in coffins!

                    BELA
No!

                    CRISWELL
Yes! My father ran a mortuary – it's an old habit!

They clink beers.]

Like an apparition, Bunny drifts among the beef carcasses with a MARIACHI BAND. *He sings in Spanish. Tor is startled to see him.*

                    TOR
Mister Bunny, what is wronk? I heard your were becomink lady!

                    BUNNY
Oh, that. Mexico was a nightmare: we got in a car accident, he was killed, our luggage was stolen, the surgeon turned out to be a quack . . .
                    (he sighs)
If it hadn't been for these mariachis, I don't know *how* I would've survived.

* Cut from completed film.

103

EXT. MEAT-PACKING PLANT – SAME TIME

Outside, Vampira and two GIRLFRIENDS *walk up. They peer at a tin sign.*

GIRLFRIEND #1
'McCoy Meat Packing'? Are you sure there's a party here?

VAMPIRA
(*holding an invitation*)
Yeah, I got this invitation. It's a *Bride of the Atom* party, whatever that means.

They open the large steel door and inside is the wild bash.]

INT. PARTY – SAME TIME

Across the room, Paul and Conrad chat.

PAUL MARCO
Glen or Glenda, now that was a hell of a picture.

CONRAD
Well, this new one's gonna be a hundred times better.

PAUL MARCO
Is that possible?

Dolores overhears this. She stares in disbelief.

AT THE TURNTABLE:

Someone changes the record. Brassy stripper music begins.

A door opens and Ed struts out, in full gaudy drag.

Everybody turns. They start whistling and hollering.

Ed grins, and starts into a wacky bump-and-grind.

VOICE
Go, baby, go!

Bunny runs up and sticks a dollar bill between Ed's fake tits.† *People laugh hysterically.*

---

* Cut from completed film.
† In the completed film Criswell slips the bill into the top of Ed's stockings.

Dolores is appalled.

Ed shimmies to the music, blowing kisses all around. *[He sees Vampira and waves.

Vampira's jaw drops in recognition.

> VAMPIRA
> I don't believe it. It's *him*!]

Ed sashays up to Bela and dances a few steps with him. The music is building to a climax. Ed hurries off to center stage – and as the music ends, he does a final swing of his hips, then suddenly yanks out his teeth!

This brings down the house. Everyone stamps their feet and claps crazily.

ANGLE – DOLORES:

Everyone, except Dolores. Suddenly, she explodes.

> DOLORES
> You people are *insane*! Take a look around – you're all *freaks*!

The room quiets. Dolores has snapped.

> You're wasting your lives making *shit*! Nobody cares! These movies are *terrible*!
> (*beat*)
> I can't take it any longer!

The group is shocked. Nobody speaks.

Dolores runs out of the party.

Ed just stands, dumbstruck. Then he chases after her, in his high heels and dress.

EXT. MEAT-PACKING PLANT – SAME TIME

Dolores runs across the parking lot, in tears. Ed catches up with her.

> ED
> Dolores, wait!

* Cut from completed film.

                              DOLORES
Ed, it's over. I need a normal life.

                                ED
                              (*hurt*)
Did you really mean those things you said . . .?

Dolores stops.

                              DOLORES
I'm tired of living on the fringe.

                                ED
But you used to say –

                              DOLORES
Ed . . . I just stuck it out so you could finish your movie.
                              (*pause*)
Now that it's done, so am I.

*She turns and walks away. Ed is crushed. He stands motionless, in his
dress, in the dark.*

CUT TO:

*[INT. ED'S NEW APARTMENT – DAY

*Ed's new home is a single apartment, still filled with moving boxes.
Half-eaten plates of food are scattered about. Ed lies asleep in bed,
unshaven, in the middle of the day.*

The phone rings. Ed awakens and woozily answers it.

                                ED
Yeah . . .

                                TOR
                            (*on phone*)
Ed, dit I wake you? It's two in avternoon.

                                ED
No, I was just doin' a little work . . .

---

* Cut from completed film.

TOR
(*on phone*)
Bullchit! You been like dis too many days. I want to cheer you up.

EXT. TOR'S HOUSE – NIGHT

Ed drives his Nash through a tract Valley neighborhood and reaches Tor's little house. Ed gets out, still looking groggy. He walks up the tulip-lined path and rings the doorbell. Clanging Swedish chimes bong inside.

The door flies open and Tor appears, beaming.

TOR
Edvard, you come!

Tor gives Ed a back-breaking hug.

INT. TOR'S HOUSE – SAME TIME

Ed steps in. The house is filled with cuckoo clocks and little Swedish knick-knacks. Tor gestures proudly.

TOR
I'm so happy you visit. Meet my family! Greta, Karl and Connie!

Three colossal people lumber out. Tor has the largest family we've ever seen. Not fat – but big-boned. GRETA *is Tor's gigantic Swedish wife, and* KARL *and* CONNIE *are their two elephantine children. They ad-lib greetings: 'Hallo!' 'Welcome! 'Is a pleasure!'*

Ed cannot believe what he's seeing.

INT. DINING ROOM – NIGHT

Everyone noisily eats dinner. The table looks like a smorgasbord. Entire hams, turkeys, a full case of beer, incredible quantities are being shoveled in. Tor empties a beer in one gulp, then opens another.

CONNIE
Pass the meatballs.

KARL

This strudel is delicious, Mama.

Ed is stupefied. He picks at a little dainty serving.

TOR

Hey! You're not eatink.

ED

Uh, I don't have much of an appetite lately.

TOR

The food will make you feel bedder. Look at me – I'm da happiest guy I know!

All the Johnsons chuckle.

ED

I'd be happy too, if I had such a great family.

TOR

Don't worry. You just haven't met right woman yet.
(*beat*)
Oopsy. That cabbage goes right through me.

Tor stands and hurries from the room. Ed awkwardly makes conversation.

ED

Greta, your husband is a terrific actor. You should come down and visit the set.

GRETA

I don't think so.

ED

No, it's really no problem at all!

GRETA
(*steely*)
I do not approve of what you do with my husband Tor. He is not a monster. These horror pictures are humiliating.

Ed has no response. Suddenly – crash! There's a loud offscreen slam, falling porcelain, then Tor shouts furiously in Swedish.

TOR
(*off*)

Ouch! Goddammit!

Karl and Connie begin giggling. Ed is totally baffled.

Tor runs out, angrily holding a broken toilet seat. It is split in two.

TOR

Look, it happened again!

Ed is boggle-eyed. This house is madness.

ED

Tor, I should be getting home.

TOR

Nonsense! You must try our hot glug.

DISSOLVE TO:

INT. TOR'S HOUSE – LATER

It's very late. Tor and Ed sit in the living room, drinking from a steaming pot of hot mulled wine. They are smashed.

TOR

My friend, you think Greta is first woman I ever met? No! Many duds, before I find her.

ED

But I thought me and Dolores had something.

TOR

Forget her! Move on. A good lookink boy like you – you can have any girl you wish.

Tor finishes his glug, then his eyes roll back into his head and he falls off the couch. He starts snoring.

Ed stares at Tor, then gets up. Ed turns off the lights and goes home.

CUT TO:]

INT. ED'S APARTMENT – LATE NIGHT

Ed smokes a cigarette and watches TV.

ON THE TV:

Vampira is doing her shtick.

> VAMPIRA
> (*on TV*)
> Ooo! That was so scary, it gave me goosebumps.
>> (*someone quacks offscreen; she pretends to be angry*)
> No, dummy! I didn't say 'goose', I said 'goosebumps'. Ugh! Well, be sure to join me next week for *The Mummy's Curse*. Until then . . . pleasant nightmares.

Vampira blows a kiss, then disappears into the mist. A used-car commercial comes on abruptly.

ON ED:

He stares at the TV, then picks up the phone.

CUT TO:

INT. TV STUDIOS – SAME TIME

Vampira is walking off stage. She removes her black wig.

> VAMPIRA
> God, we need some better jokes on this show.

A PRODUCTION ASSISTANT carries over a phone.

> ASSISTANT
> Vampira, you got a phone call.

> VAMPIRA
> At this hour?
>> (*she takes the phone*)
> Hello?

> ED'S VOICE
> Vampira! Hi, this is Ed Wood.

Who?

ED'S VOICE

Ed Wood! You came to my party. I directed *Bride of the Atom*!

VAMPIRA

Oh. Yea. You.

Ed pauses, nervously.

ED'S VOICE

Well, I was wondering if maybe sometime you'd like to go out, and maybe grab some dinner.

VAMPIRA

You mean like a date? I thought you were a fag.

ED'S VOICE

Me?! No, um, I'm just a transvestite.

VAMPIRA

Isn't that the same thing?

ED'S VOICE

No, no! I like girls. So how 'bout Friday?

VAMPIRA
(*uncomfortably*)

Look, you seem like a nice guy, Ed, but you're not my type.
(*beat*)
But keep in touch. Let me know when your movie opens.

CUT BACK TO:

CU – ED:

Click. The phone hangs up. Poor Ed just sits there, forlorn.

CUT TO:

*[EXT. CITY STREET – DAY

Ed shuffles down the street, Mr Lonely Guy, feeling sorry for himself.

* Cut from completed film.

He glances in a coffee shop and sees a sweet young woman inside. Her name is NORMA MCCARTY. *She wears a bow in her hair, Mary Jane shoes, and a fuzzy white angora sweater.*

Ed's eyes widen.

INT. COFFEE SHOP – SAME TIME

Innocent Norma sits by herself, eating.

> ED'S VOICE
>
> Excuse me. Is that angora?

Norma looks up. Standing over her is Ed, smiling.

> NORMA
>
> Why . . . yes.

> ED
>
> Don't you think angora has a tactile sensuality lacking in all other clothing?

> NORMA
>
> I suppose. It's very expensive.

> ED
>
> It's made from specially bred rabbits that live in the Himalayas.

> NORMA
>
> What are you, an angora wholesaler?

> ED
>
> No, I work in pictures. I'm a director–actor–writer–producer.

> NORMA
> (*she laughs*)
>
> Ah, c'mon! Nobody does all that.

> ED
>
> Two people do. Orson Welles and me.

> NORMA
>
> Wow . . .

ED

You know, you're a very attractive girl.

Norma blushes.

NORMA

My goodness, you're embarrassing me.

ED

You shouldn't be embarrassed by the truth.
                    (*he smoothly sits down*)
Mind if I order some hotcakes . . .?

CUT TO:

INT. CRISWELL'S CADILLAC – NIGHT

*Criswell and Paul drive at night. They're dressed up. Swing music plays
on the radio.*

CRISWELL

So who's the surprise for?

PAUL MARCO

I dunno. Ed was real mysterious. All he'd say was it's a surprise
party.

CRISWELL

Isn't that like him!
                    (*beat*)
And isn't that like *us* – that we show up anyway.

They pull up to a GUARD at a gate. They're at a studio.

CRISWELL

Excuse me. We're here for the Wood party.

GUARD

They've rented Stage Twelve. Drive straight back.

INT. SOUNDSTAGE – NIGHT

*There is another rambunctious party in progress. Crêpe-paper streamers
hang down. Bela approaches Tor.*

BELA

So what are we doing here?

TOR

Nobody knows. But there's a lotta booze.

Suddenly Ed steps into the middle of the room. He's extremely handsome in his tuxedo and beaming happily.

ED

Excuse me! Could everyone please quiet down?
(*the room quiets*)
First of all, I want to thank you, all my good friends, for being here tonight. And second, if you're wondering what the big surprise is . . . well, *tonight I'm getting married*!!

The crowd is stunned.

Many people drop their glasses.

Ed proudly pulls out Norma. She's in a wedding gown.

Everybody, this is *Norma*!

ON BELA AND TOR:

They're bewildered. Bela whispers.

BELA

Who the fuck is she??

TOR

I never heard of her.

Ed walks over. He hugs Bela.

ED

And Bela, I want you to be the best man!

Bela smiles – trying to hide his total confusion.

DISSOLVE TO:

INT. SOUNDSTAGE – LATER

The wedding is in progress. The crowd is seated. A MINISTER *performs the ceremony with Ed and Norma.*

> MINISTER
> . . . Norma, do you promise to love, honor and cherish . . .

IN THE CROWD:

Everybody is quietly gossiping.

> BUNNY
> I didn't even know he had a girlfriend.

> PAUL MARCO
> (*he taps him on the shoulder*)
> I hear she's an actress who gave him money.

> CONRAD
> Nah, I heard she's his childhood sweetheart from Poughkeepsie.

> CRISWELL
> I predict it's Dolores in a mask.

AT THE ALTAR:

The Minister is speaking to Ed.

> MINISTER
> . . . in sickness and in health, till death do you part?

> ED
> I do.

> MINISTER
> (*he smiles*)
> Then I now pronounce you man and wife.

Ed kisses Norma.

The crowd doesn't applaud. They're too baffled by this whole event.

DISSOLVE TO:

INT. SOUNDSTAGE – LATER

At the reception, everyone's drinking and dancing. Ed proudly introduces Norma to his buddies.

> ED

Norma, this is Bela – Bela, this is Norma. Norma, this is Tor –
Tor, this is Norma. Norma, this is Paul – Paul, this is Norma.

> PAUL MARCO
> (*he can't resist*)

So how long have you known Eddie?

> NORMA
> (*sweetly*)

Since Tuesday.

Criswell grabs Ed and pulls him aside.

> CRISWELL

Edward, are you sure you know what you're doing?

> ED

Yeah. It seems a little crazy, but sometimes *you just know*. She's
perfect for me.

Outside, a car honks.

> ED

Oop, that's our cue!
> (*to Norma*)

Honey, we gotta go. *Goodbye, everybody!*

Ed and Norma run out the door. The crowd hurries after them.

EXT. SOUNDSTAGE – SAME TIME

*Ed and Norma jump into his Nash. It says 'Just Married' and is
festooned with dangling tin cans. The car screeches away. The cans rattle
noisily, then slowly fade into the distance . . .*

CUT TO:

EXT. MOTEL – NIGHT

*We're at a desert roadside motel, the San Bernardino Arms. A 'Vacancy'
light flashes.*

INT. MOTEL ROOM – SAME TIME

Ed excitedly carries Norma over the threshold. He throws her onto the bed and they start ardently making out.

> NORMA
> Eddie, I'm just a small-town girl. I've never done this before.

> ED
> *(kissing her)*
> Don't worry, I'll teach you.

He helps her remove her wedding dress. She is very shy.

> NORMA
> Be understanding. I don't know anything.

Ed removes his jacket, then gestures to his shirt. Norma nervously starts unbuttoning it.

Ed bites his lip in anticipation.

Norma opens his shirt . . . and inside, Ed is wearing a bra!

Norma is horrified.

> NORMA
> What the heck is this?!!

> ED
> Honey, I have a little secret to share with you.

CUT TO:

EXT. MOTEL – SAME TIME

There's a loud woman's scream.

Then the door slams open and Norma runs out hysterically, clutching her dress about her.

> NORMA
> Stay away from me! You're perverted!

Ed runs out after her.

> ED
> Please, be compassionate. I'm your husband!

No you're not! This marriage was never consummated. I'm getting an annulment!

CUT TO:

EXT. LOS ANGELES STREETS — LATE NIGHT

Ed drives sadly through the streets, alone. His car still says 'Just Married' and the tin cans rattle behind him.

CUT TO:]

INT. ED'S APARTMENT — LATE NIGHT

Ed is awakened by a phone call from Bela.

EXT. BELA'S HOUSE — LATE NIGHT

Ed's car pulls up. Ed stumbles out, yanks off the tin cans and throws them in someone's trash.

Ed despondently approaches Bela's. Inside, a light glows and the dogs bark.

Ed is relieved. Bela's awake. He bangs on the door.

ED

Bela, let me in! Bela, it's Eddie.

He keeps banging. Finally the door opens — and Bela stands there, shakily waving a gun! Bela is doped up, glassy-eyed, and disturbingly haggard.

BELA

Why are you here?

ED

Shit! Bela, what's with the gun?

BELA

*[Why aren't you on your honeymoon? Where's Myrna?

ED

Norma. She changed her mind. She doesn't wanna marry me.
(*beat*)

* Cut from completed film.

118

Can you put down the gun?

Bela weakly lowers the gun.]

INT. BELA'S HOUSE – SAME TIME

Ed walks in, in a near-stupor. Needles and drug paraphernalia are scattered about.

>   ED
>
> What are you doing?

>   BELA
>
> I was thinking about killing myself.

>   ED
>
> *[Jesus Christ, what an evening.]
> *(he looks around)*
> What happened?

>   BELA
>   *(near tears)*
> Eddie, I received a letter from the government. They're cutting off my unemployment. That's all I've got. Without it, I can't pay the rent . . .

>   ED
>
> Don't you have any savings?

>   BELA
>
> I'm obsolete. I have nothing to live for. Tonight, I should die.
>   *(distraught)*
> And you should come with me.

Frail Bela points the gun at Ed. Ed is terrified.

>   ED
>
> Buddy, I don't know if that's such a good idea.

>   BELA
>
> It'll be wonderful. We'll be at peace. In the afterlife, you don't have to worry about finding work.

* Cut from completed film.

ED

Bela, I'm on your side. C'mon give me the gun . . .
> (*he cautiously steps forward*)

If you give me the gun, I'll make you a drink. What are you drinking?

BELA

Formaldehyde.

Ed stares in anguish.

ED

Straight up or on the rocks?

Bela drops the gun. He starts weeping.

Ed walks over and hugs the shaking old man.

Don't worry.

BELA

I'm sorry, Eddie. I'm so sorry.

ED

Don't worry. Everything's gonna be all right.

CUT TO:

*[EXT. HOSPITAL – STILL LATER THAT NIGHT

Ed's car pulls up at the South Metropolitan State Hospital. It's a grim, unwelcoming edifice.

Ed helps weak Bela from the car. They look at each other, then Ed gingerly leads Bela in.]

INT. HOSPITAL – SAME TIME

The lobby is clammy and dim. Ed and Bela reach the desk. A NURSE *looks up, startled.*

NURSE

My goodness, you gave me the willies. You look like that Dracula guy.

*Cut from completed film.

                    BELA
                 (*very somber*)
My name is Bela Lugosi. I wish to commit myself.

                    NURSE
For what reason?

                    BELA
I have been a drug addict for twenty years. I need help . . .

The nurse nods. She takes Bela's arm and leads him away. Bela glances at Ed, then steps through a wide door. As it swings shut, we see a DOCTOR *walk over and shake Bela's hand.*

Ed stares at the door, dazed by all that's happened. He sits down in the chair, exhausted.

Ed's eyes slowly close, and he falls asleep . . .

   DISSOLVE TO:

INT. HOSPITAL — MORNING

Ed is still asleep, but now sunlight beats in.

Ed stirs and wakes up. He looks around groggily, and sitting across from him is a woman, knitting. This is KATHY O'HARA, *twenty-six, solid, reflective, with a dry sense of humor. Ed peers at her.*

                 *[ED
Hello.

                   KATHY
Hello.
                 (*beat*)
You're sleeping in a tuxedo.

                    ED
I got married last night.

                   KATHY
Oh. Congratulations.

* In the completed film, the dialogue between Ed and Norma (see page 112) was used here.

                    121

                              ED

The marriage already ended.

                            KATHY

Oh. My condolences.]

Ed watches her knit.

                              ED

What are you making?

                            KATHY

Booties for my father. He gets cold in the hospital.

                              ED

How long's he been here?

                            KATHY

This is my thirteenth pair.

Ed nods. He spots the Doctor walk by.

                              ED

Excuse me.
                    (*he runs to the doctor*)
Doctor? I'm with Mr Lugosi. How is he?

                            DOCTOR

Well . . . there's a lot of junk in his system for such an old man.
Apparently, he was addicted to morphine, tried to kick it, and got
readdicted to methadone.

                              ED

Will he be okay?

                            DOCTOR

We'll do our best.

DISSOLVE TO:

INT. HOSPITAL CORRIDOR – NIGHT

*We are outside Bela's room. He can be glimpsed inside, strapped to the
bed and screaming in pain. He is going through painful withdrawal and
shakes horribly.*

DISSOLVE TO:

INT. HOSPITAL LOBBY — ANOTHER DAY

Ed strides into the hospital, wearing different clothes and carrying a box of chocolates. He waves at the nurse.

> ED
>
> Hi, Lillian.

> NURSE
> (*she smiles*)
>
> Hi, Ed. Boy, he's got a lot of visitors today.

> ED
>
> He does?

Ed is puzzled, He hurries back.

INT. HOSPITAL CORRIDOR — DAY

A crowd of NEWSPAPER REPORTERS *and* PHOTOGRAPHERS *overflow Bela's room. Ed is astonished.*

> ED
>
> What's going on here?! Excuse me!

INT. HOSPITAL ROOM — SAME TIME

Decrepit Bela is propped up in his bed, as the mob of reporters throw questions at him and snap shots: 'Bela, how long have you been a junkie??' 'Bela, look this way!'

Ed pushes through angrily.

> ED
>
> Everybody out! This is a hospital! Get out of here.

Ed forces them out, then slams the door.

What happened?!

BELA
(*in a hoarse whisper*)
Isn't it wonderful? After all these years, the press is showing an interest in Bela Lugosi.

ED
(*surprised*)
Bela, they're parasites! They just want to exploit you.

BELA
Fine. Let them! There is no such thing as bad press. A man from New York said he's putting me on the front page! First celebrity to ever check into rehab.
(*he smiles feebly*)
When I get out of here, I will be healthy. Strong! I will be primed for my comeback!

Bela starts coughing heavily. Ed stares sadly.

DISSOLVE TO:

INT. LOBBY — ANOTHER DAY

Ed sits tensely in the lobby, holding vigil. Kathy O'Hara walks by.

KATHY
Oh, it's you again.

ED
Oh, hi.

KATHY
You look beat.

ED
I am. How's your father?

KATHY
He's better. Thank you for asking.
(*pause*)
How's your friend?

ED
Not good . . .

Kathy reaches for her purse and pulls out two black booties.

> KATHY
> Well, I made him some booties to cheer him up.
> > (*beat*)
> They're black – to match his cape.

She smiles.

Ed slowly smiles in response. But this isn't his normal slick smile. It's gentler. Sincere.

> ED
> Would you maybe like to get a coffee . . .?

DISSOLVE TO:

INT. HOSPITAL CORRIDOR – DAY

Ed and the Doctor stand in a doorway, talking.

> DOCTOR
> We thought Mr Lugosi was insured through his union.

> ED
> Isn't he?

> DOCTOR
> No. They say his eligibility ran out years ago.

> ED
> Look, he doesn't have any money . . . but I'll give you everything I've got. I have a few hundred dollars.

The Doctor shakes his head grimly.

> DOCTOR
> That won't even begin to cover it. He's going to have to leave.

INT. BELA'S HOSPITAL ROOM – DAY

Bela lies sleeping in bed, pasty and pale. Newspaper clippings of his hospital stay are tacked up.

Ed anxiously tiptoes in. He quietly speaks.

> ED

Bela, wake up.

Bela stirs lethargically. Ed puts on a fake smile.

I've got some good news. The doctor says you're all better. You can come home.

> BELA
> (*so weak, he's barely audible*)

Really? I don't feel so great.

> ED

No, you look good. And the tests came back fine.
> (*a poignant pause*)

C'mon . . .

Ed gingerly helps Bela up.

EXT. HOSPITAL – DAY

Bela slowly gets into Ed's car.

> BELA

Eddie, I wanna make another picture. When are we gonna make another picture?

> ED

Soon, Bela . . . Soon.

CUT TO:

*[INT. CAMERA RENTAL HOUSE – DAY

Ed is desperately trying to cut a deal with the OLD MANAGER.

> ED

Please, I just need it for one afternoon!

> OLD MANAGER

Ed, if I cut a deal for you, I gotta cut one for everybody.

---

* Cut from completed film.

ED

This is different! It'll mean so much to me. All I need is a camera and a tripod. No lights, no sound. Nothin' fancy.

OLD MANAGER

And that's it?

ED

And one roll of film.
The old guy gives Ed a tough look.

CUT TO:]

EXT. BEL'S HOUSE – DAY

Bela is dressed in his Sunday finest, standing in front of his little house. He wears a cloak and a wide-brimmed hat.

BELA

This is so exciting. Another production!

WE WIDEN:
Out on the lawn . . . is just Ed. With the camera.

So Eddie, don't we need a sound crew?

ED

No, this is just the second unit. We'll do the main footage later.

BELA

Oh. So what is the scene about?

ED
(*improvising*)

Uh . . . you're a very important and respected man. You're leaving your house . . . and you're in a hurry to a big social event.

Bela nods. He mulls this over.

BELA

Okay. But what if I'm not in *too* big a hurry? What if I take a moment to slow down and savor the beauty of life? To smell a flower?

ED
(he smiles)
That's great. Let's do a take.

WIDE:

Bela goes in the front door. Ed gets behind the camera, then turns it on.

Okay, roll camera! Rolling. Scene One, Take One!
(pause)
And . . . action!

There's a moment. And then Bela slowly steps outside, calm, dignified, walking with a cane. He looks about – and then something catches his eye. He leans down and picks a flower.

Bela smells the flower, then abruptly drops it. He starts crying. A pause, and then he composes himself. The old man slowly shuffles out of frame.

Ed peers emotionally from behind the camera.

And cut . . .

BELA
Eddie, how was I?

ED
(quiet)
Perfect.

Bela is pleased.

BELA
*[Good.
(beat)
Now what about my close-up?

CUT TO:

EXT. HOLLYWOOD DUPLEX – DUSK

Ed's Nash convertible pulls up outside a neat little duplex in a nice neighborhood. Ed is dressed-up for a date. He checks his hair nervously in

* Cut from completed film.

128

the mirror, revealing an anxious boyishness we've never seen before.

Ed carries a bouquet of flowers to the front door. He rings the bell. Kathy opens the door. She looks very pretty in a full skirt with a crinolin.

> KATHY
>
> Oh, flowers! I didn't know you were so traditional.

> ED
> (*a little embarrassed*)
>
> I just picked them up on the way over . . .

> KATHY
>
> They're very nice.
> (*she smiles sweetly*)
> Let me get my coat.]

EXT. CARNIVAL – NIGHT

Ed and Kathy are at a tattered traveling carnival. Rattling steel rides and flashing lights spin about them. They stroll through the crowds, eating cotton candy. Kathy wears one of Ed's flowers on her dress.

> KATHY
>
> So have you always lived in LA?

> ED
>
> No. I'm from back East. You know, All-American small town . . . everybody knew everybody, I was a Boy Scout, my dad worked for the post office . . .

> KATHY
>
> Sounds like you lived in Grovers Corners.

INT. SPOOK HOUSE – NIGHT

Ed and Kathy ride through the old mechanical spook house.

> KATHY
>
> Did you find it boring?

> ED
>
> Nah, 'cause I had my comic books. And I read pulp magazines.

And I listened to the radio dramas . . .

A wooden witch jumps out at them. They ignore it.

> KATHY
> Oh, I loved those shows! *Inner Sanctum . . . The Shadow* –

> ED
> (*getting excited*)
> Yeah! Don't forget *Mercury Theater* . . . And then every Saturday,
> I'd go to the little movie theater down the street. I even started
> ushering there.

A creaky ghost flies overhead.

> KATHY
> You're not gonna believe the first picture I ever saw. Your
> friend's.

> ED
> What do you mean?

> KATHY
> *Dracula.*

Ed freaks out.

> ED
> That's *incredible*! That's the first picture *I* ever saw!!

WIDE:

Mechanical bats drop down and flap around them.

> KATHY
> That *is* incredible!
> (*beat*)
> You know, I had to sleep with the lights on for a week after seeing
> that movie.

> ED
> I had to sleep with the lights on for a month.
> (*he smiles*)
> But I never missed a Lugosi picture after that.

KATHY

A few years ago, I actually saw him do *Dracula* live. I thought he
was much scarier in person.

CU – ED:

He stares at Kathy in wonder. He is overcome.

★[Their car smashes through the tin exit doors.]

EXT. SPOOK HOUSE – SAME TIME

Ed and Kathy's little car comes to a stop. He gets very serious.

ED

Kathy, I'm about to tell you something I've never told any girl on a
first date. But I think it's important that you know.
(*beat*)
I like to wear women's clothes.

KATHY

Huh?

ED

I like to wear women's clothes: panties, brassières, sweaters,
pumps . . . it's just something I do. And I can't believe I'm telling
you, but I really like you, and I don't want it getting in the way
down the road.

Kathy is amazed. She contemplates all this.

KATHY

Does this mean you don't like sex with girls?

ED

No! I love sex with girls.

KATHY

Oh. Okay.

ED
(*surprised*)

Okay?

★ In the completed film their car breaks down and they're stuck inside the spook house.

Kathy slyly grins.

KATHY

Okay.

Ed grins back. A moment.

CUT TO:

INT. ED'S HOUSE – DAY

Ed is on the telephone.

*[SPLIT SCREEN *with Vampira.*]

ED
(*on phone*)

Vampira! Hi, it's Ed Wood.

VAMPIRA
(*on phone*)

Ed, I told you, I *don't* wanna go out!

ED

No, don't worry, I moved on. I was just calling to see if you want to attend the world première of my new film, *Bride of the Monster*.

VAMPIRA
(*confused*)

Didn't you just make one called *Bride of the Atom*?

ED

It's the same film. But the distributor wanted a punchier title. C'mon! It's gonna be a big event – we're going all out! Bela, Tor and Cris are coming. You'll have fun!

Vampira rolls her eyes.

CUT TO:

* This device not used in completed film.

*[EXT. NEIGHBORHOOD MOVIE THEATER – NIGHT

Hundreds of KIDS *and* TEENAGERS *enter a dilapidated second-run theater. A banner says:* ' "BRIDE OF THE MONSTER" WORLD PREMIÈRE! CELEBRITIES IN PERSON!']

EXT. DARK CITY STREET – SAME TIME

An antique limousine hearse drives down a dingy street.

*[INT. HEARSE – SAME TIME

Ed drives. Tor, ill Bela, Vampira and Criswell are crammed in with him, along with bewildered Kathy.

Everyone is dressed in gaudy 'scary' outfits. Tor wears his frightening white contact lenses.

> TOR
> My eyes are killink me.

> ED
> Don't worry. We're almost there.

> BELA
> (*still hoarse*)
> Eddie, where are we? We passed that carwash twenty minutes ago.

> CRISWELL
> I predict we're lost.

> VAMPIRA
> (*to Bela*)
> Hey! You wanna watch the hands??

Bela sheepishly removes his hand from her thigh.

> BELA
> Sorry . . .

* Cut from completed film.

ED
(*he looks around, baffled*)
Has anyone ever been to Downey?

INT. MOVIE THEATER – SAME TIME

The audience is so restless, they're practically rioting. They clap and chant angrily.

A fat patronizing MANAGER *steps on stage.*

THEATER MANAGER
Children, if you don't calm down, there won't be the entertainment.

ANGRY KID
It was supposed to start an hour ago!]

INT. HEARSE – SAME TIME

Tempers are flaring.

TOR
My eyes are burnink.

KATHY
Hey look! There's the theater.

TOR
Where? I can't see nothink!

EXT. THEATER – SAME TIME

The hearse pulls up. A FRANTIC USHER *runs over.*

FRANTIC USHER
Thank God you're here! They're tearing the place apart!

The gang awkwardly steps out of the hearse. Tor gets out and blindly walks straight into a lamp post. Whack! He yelps.

TOR
Ow!

Bela moves slowly, he's very feeble. Vampira smooths out her slinky black dress, then puts her arm around Bela to help him.

> FRANTIC USHER

C'mon! This way!

INT. THEATER — SAME TIME

Criswell points Tor in the right direction and the group stumbles in. Ed escorts excited Kathy.

> KATHY

I've never been to a première before.

The Usher opens the auditorium doors.

INSIDE:

It's pandemonium. People are screaming and shouting. Kids run up and down, on top of the chairs.

Bela, Tor, Vampira and Criswell are alarmed.

The lights dim on and off. Scratchy spooky music blasts over the sound system.

> ED

Wow. Go knock 'em dead!

Criswell pushes blind Tor towards the stage. Tor sticks out his arms and scarily staggers down the aisle. Criswell nervously follows. Vampira escorts Bela.

The crowd boos. They pelt our gang with popcorn.

Tor growls like a monster. Kids laugh and jeer.

ON ED AND KATHY:

At the back, Ed speaks in a frightening manner into a microphone:

> ED
> (amplified)

Ooooo! At the stroke of midnight, the witching hour, the ghouls arise from the *dead!*

*[DOWN THE AISLE:

Tor slips on some butter. He tumbles and falls.

A WOMAN'S VOICE *cackles.*

> WOMAN'S VOICE
> It's the blind leading the blind!

Tor staggers to his feet. All disoriented, he starts walking in the wrong direction and falls over a chair. People heckle.

Criswell quickly helps him up.

> TOR
> Dis is a nightmare.

> CRISWELL
> It's showbiz.

Criswell pushes Tor in the right direction. Some roughnecks knock down Criswell and snatch his wallet.

A MEAN BOY *jumps on his chair, ripping the stuffing out of the seat. He throws the fibers in the air, and they float over Bela and Vampira.*

> BELA
> What is that?

> VAMPIRA
> I think they're getting ready to burn this place down.]

A HIGH-SCHOOL PUNK *runs up and grabs Vampira's breasts.*

> *[HIGH-SCHOOL PUNK
> Hey Vampira, how 'bout a little love?

> VAMPIRA
> Fuck off!

She impulsively swings her arm and slams the kid.

ON STAGE:

The manager pleads to the mob.

---

* Cut from completed film.

Children please! Be calm!

Somebody throws a bottle and hits him on the head. He goes down.]

WIDE:

The lights suddenly go off. Some girls scream.

Ed's panicked. He grabs Kathy and runs down to his friends.

ED

C'mon! We're getting the hell out of here!

Ed rounds up Bela, Tor, Criswell and Vampira.

The crowd boos louder. Blind Tor is totally confused.

TOR

What is happening?

ED

We're escaping!

The group runs up the aisle and leaves. As the doors close, Bride of the Monster *starts unspooling on the screen.*

EXT. THEATER – SAME TIME

The gang frantically runs out, scared for their lives.

They look over. Some JUVENILE DELINQUENTS *are stripping the hearse.*

*[VAMPIRA

We're gonna die.]

The theater doors crash open. The angry mob pours out.

Ed spins wildly around . . . and sees a cab approaching.

ED

Stop!

KATHY

Stop!

*Cut from completed film.

137

Kathy runs frenziedly into the street and throws herself at the cab. It screeches to a halt.

Everybody sprints over and jumps in. The cab roars away.

INT. CAB – SAME TIME

All of them are breathing heavily. They watch in the rear window as they drive away from the rampage.

A nervous silence. Until Bela speaks.

> BELA
> Now *that* was a première.

All of them laugh.

CUT TO:

EXT. HOLLYWOOD BOULEVARD – DAY

Bela and Ed stroll down the street in high spirits.

> BELA
> Last night was quite a romp.

> ED
> Did you see that kid grab Vampira's tits?

> BELA
> I envied him.
>> (*he chuckles*)
> Hell, I envied you too, having a girlfriend that would jump in front of a car like that.

> ED
> Yeah, she's really somethin'.

> BELA
> I know none of *my* wives would've.

Ed laughs. Bela puffs his cigar.

> BELA
> Eddie, I want to thank you. These last few days have been a good time.

ED

I just wish you coulda seen the movie.

BELA

No problem. I know it by heart . . .

Bela stops walking. And in a booming, theatrical voice, he suddenly launches into his impassioned climactic speech from Bride of the Monster.

'Home. I have no home. Hunted . . . despised . . . living like an animal – the jungle is my home! But I will show the world that I can be its master. I shall perfect my own race of people . . . a race of atomic supermen that will conquer the world!'

Ed is touched.

A few people around them applaud.

Bela's face lights up proudly. An awed Midwestern TOURIST *hands him a pen and paper.*

TOURIST

Mr Lugosi, could I have your autograph.

BELA

Certainly.

TOURIST

Boy, that was incredible. You're just as good an actor as you always were.

Bela puffs out his chest majestically.

BELA

Better.
(*beat*)
I'm seventy-four, but I don't know it. If the brain is young, then the spirit is still vigorous . . . like a young man.

Bela turns and smiles warmly at Ed.

Ed smiles back.

CUT TO:

INT. ED'S KITCHEN – NIGHT

*[*Ed and Kathy stand in his kitchen, making dinner. She sticks her finger in a pot.*

                         KATHY
    Ed, this spaghetti sauce is delicious.

                          ED
    Thanks. It's actually the only thing I know how to make.
                    (*he motions*)
    Hey, can you grab the strainer?

She holds a strainer. Ed pours the spaghetti over it.]

Suddenly the phone rings. Ed groans.

    Ugh! Always at the wrong time.
                    (*he answers the phone*)
    Hello?

Ed listens.

And then, gets a very somber expression.

    Oh no . . .

Ed hangs up the phone. He looks pained.

                         KATHY
    What was that?

                          ED
                       (*quiet*)

    Bela died.

    CUT TO:

INT. FUNERAL HOME – DAY

It's Bela's funeral.

Ed sits crying in the front row, with Kathy at his side.

All Bela's friends are there. They're very subdued.

* In the completed film, Ed is reading a story to Kathy.

THE CASKET:

Bela lies inside, made up in his full Dracula outfit. His hair is dyed black and he wears the famous cape.

EXT. HOLY CROSS CEMETERY — DAY

On a grassy hill, Bela is laid to rest. The small crowd of mourners stands silhouetted against the dark gray clouds.

The coffin is lowered into the ground. Ed stands at the front, silently watching.

AT A DISTANCE:

A few tabloid PHOTOGRAPHERS *snap pictures.*

> PHOTOGRAPHER #1
> Whose crazy idea was it to bury him in the cape?

> PHOTOGRAPHER #1
> I heard it was in the will. It was how he wanted to be remembered.

CUT TO:

INT. SCREENING ROOM — DAY

Ed is alone in a darkened screening room, depressed.

ONSCREEN:

The last footage of Bela is playing: Bela stumbles around in front of his house and smells the flower.

*[Ed drinks out of a flask.]

The film runs out. A VOICE *comes over a loudspeaker.*

> VOICE
> Do you want me to run it again?

Ed silently nods.

DISSOLVE TO:

* Cut from completed film.

*[INT. ED'S APARTMENT – NIGHT

Ed's apartment has gone to hell. Ed is in a robe, unshaven and clutching a bottle of whiskey. Newspapers are everywhere. Bela's and Ed's dogs eat out of the trash.

Kathy tries to straighten things up. Ed stares listlessly.

                    ED
I'd seen him in a coffin so many times, I expected him to jump out . . .

                    KATHY
Ed, you've got to snap out of this. Bela's dead – *you're not!*

                    ED
I might as well be. I made shitty movies that nobody wanted to see.
                    (*beat*)
I blew it. All he wanted was a comeback . . . that last glory . . .

                    KATHY
Well you tried –

                    ED
                    (*angry*)
I was a fuckin' *hack!* I let people recut the movies, cast their relatives . . .
                    (*beat*)
I let Bela down . . .

CUT TO:]

EXT. ED'S APARTMENT BUILDING – DAY

A new Studebaker pulls up. A bumper sticker says 'JESUS SAVES'

A man in a plain brown suit steps out. This is J. EDWARD REYNOLDS, *fifty, Ed's sanctimonious Southern Christian landlord. Reynolds assertively bangs on Ed's front door.*

                    REYNOLDS
Mr Wood?!

* Cut from completed film.

142

                              ED
                            (*off*)
Hruphh . . .?

                           REYNOLDS
Mr Wood, this is Mr Reynolds, your landlord. Could you please
open up?

The door opens a crack. Bleary Ed peers out.

                              ED
Yeah . . .?

                           REYNOLDS
Mr Wood, you have bounced your third and final rent check.

                              ED
                      (*he sloppily lies*)
I'm real sorry. My stockbroker must have transferred the wrong
account . . . C'mon in, I'll write you another one.

INT. APARTMENT – SAME TIME

*Ed motions Reynolds in. Reynolds peers unsurely at the tornado inside.
Then he notices a framed one-sheet for 'BRIDE OF THE MONSTER.'
Reynolds admires it.*

                           REYNOLDS
Ah, so you're in the picture business?

                              ED
                    (*rummaging for a check*)
You could say that –

                           REYNOLDS
I'm interested in the picture business. My associates and I wish to
produce a series of uplifting religions films, on the Apostles. But
unfortunately, we don't have enough money.

                              ED
                         (*distracted*)
Raising money is tough.

REYNOLDS

Oh! Our church has the money for one film. We just don't have it for all twelve . . .

ANGLE – ED:

His eyes suddenly pop.

The color comes back to his face. A plan is quickly boiling over inside Ed's head. He starts feverishly pacing around.

ED

Okay – you know what you do? You produce a film in a commercially proven genre. And after it's a hit, you take the profits from *that*, and make the twelve Apostles' movies.

REYNOLDS

Would that work?

ED

Absolutely! You see this script . . .?

Ed randomly grabs a script off the messy floor, then glances down to see which one he picked up. It says Graverobbers from Outer Space.

ED

Graverobbers from Outer Space! It's *money in the bank*.

REYNOLDS

Graverobbers from *what*??

ED

From outer space! It's science-fiction. *Very* big with the kids! If you make this picture, you'll have enough money to finance a *hundred* religious films!
                    (*beat*)
And pay my back rent from the profits.

Reynolds scratches his head.

REYNOLDS

I don't know . . . this is all a lot to absorb.

ED

It's a guaranteed blockbuster!

Um, I understand that this science fiction is popular – but don't
the big hits always have big stars?

ED
(*in a frenzy*)
Yeah, well we've *got* a big star! Bela Lugosi!!

REYNOLDS
(*mystified*)
Lugosi??! Didn't he pass on?

Ed grins maniacally. He grabs a small reel of 35mm film.

ED
Yes, but I've got the last footage he ever shot!

REYNOLDS
Hmm. It doesn't look like very much.

ED
It's plenty! It's the acorn that will grow a great oak. I'll just find a
double to finish his scenes, and we'll release it as 'Bela Lugosi's
Final Film'!!!

A beat. Reynolds stares, intrigued . . .

CUT TO:

INT. ED'S APARTMENT – LATER

The place is cleaned up. Ed shouts excitedly into the phone.

ED
Bunny! We're making another film! Yeah – I got the Baptist
Church of Beverly Hills to put up the cash!

Paul sticks his head in.

PAUL MARCO
Ed, I got the Lugosi lookalikes outside.

ED
Great! Bring 'em in! Bunny, I gotta run.

Ed hangs up.

Paul leads in three men. They look nothing like Bela. One is a HOMELESS BUM, *one is a* SHORT FAT MAN *and one is* CHINESE.

Ed inspects them.

> ED
>
> Hmm. Too tall . . . too short . . .
> > (*he glances at the Chinese guy*)
> And this guy doesn't work at all.

> PAUL MARCO
>
> Well, I was thinkin' like, when Bela played *Fu Manchu*.

> ED
>
> That was Karloff.
> > (*beat*)
> Paul, you gotta try harder. I don't want this film to be half-assed.
> This time, we go for the quality.

Paul turns to go.

> ED
>
> And by the way, keep Sunday free. The producers want all of us
> to get baptized.

CUT TO:

INT. KATHY'S APARTMENT – DAY

Kathy reads a newspaper while knitting an angora sweater. Ed is
typing deliriously fast – in one of his artistic fevers.*

> ED
>
> You know, when you rewrite a script, it just gets better and
> better!

> †KATHY
>
> Do you want your buttons on the left or the right?

---

* In the completed film Kathy is making the flying saucers for the film.
† Cut from completed film.

146

                           ED

The left. It's more natural.
                    (*he squints at his script*)
Hey, I've got a scene where the aliens have the ultimate bomb.
What would that be made of?

                         KATHY

Uh, atomic energy?

                           ED

No. They're beyond that! They're smarter than the humans.
What's *more* advanced?

                         KATHY

Dynamite.

                           ED

No, *bigger*! What's the biggest energy??

                         KATHY

The sun.

                           ED
                       (*ecstatic*)
Yes! *Bingo*! Solar energy! Oh, that's gonna seem so scientific.
                    (*he resumes typing*)]
This movie's gonna be the ultimate Ed Wood film. *No
compromises.*

Kathy suddenly jumps up, shocked.

                         KATHY

Oh my God. Look at this!

She runs over and shows Ed the newspaper.

INSERT – THE NEWSPAPER

A small headline says 'VAMPIRA REVEALED TO BE RED.' *Underneath
is the story:* 'Channel 7 has fired popular horror hostess Vampira, after
learning of her suspected communist leanings . . .'

ON ED AND KATHY:

They're astonished.

                              ED
Those assholes.

                              KATHY
The poor girl's out of a job.

                              ED
Yeah . . .
                    (*he looks up*)
I should give her a call.

CUT TO:

INT. COFFEE SHOP — DAY

Ed and Kathy sit with a shaken-up Vampira.

                              ED
I'm really sorry . . .

                           VAMPIRA
It's terrible. People won't even return my calls. It's like I don't
exist.

                              ED
I know what *that*'s like.
                    (*he pulls out his script*)
Anyway, I brought a copy of the script. You would play the
'Ghoul's Wife.'

                           VAMPIRA
                      (*she grimaces*)
The *Ghoul's Wife*?! God, I can't believe I'm doing this . . .

                           KATHY
You should feel lucky. Ed's the only guy in town who doesn't pass
judgment on people.

                              ED
                      (*he laughs*)
Hell, if I did, I wouldn't have any friends.

Vampira smiles uncomfortably.

                              148

Look . . . would it be possible to make the 'Ghoul's Wife' a little less prominent, so people won't really notice me in the movie?

ED

You don't wanna be noticed?

VAMPIRA

Exactly. Hey, how 'bout this – what if I don't have any lines? I'll do the part mute!

Kathy suddenly sees someone.

KATHY

Look, it's Dr Tom.

(*she shouts*)

Hey, Dr Tom!

ED

Who's Dr Tom?

KATHY

My chiropractor!

DR. TOM MASON, *a tall, slender thirty-five-year-old chiropractor, strides over. He smiles.*

DR MASON

Kathy, how are you?! You're looking in alignment today.

KATHY

Actually, my neck's a little funny.

DR MASON

Oh! Let me fix that.

Dr Mason grabs Kathy's neck and cracks it loudly.

ON ED:

Ed stares at the Doctor in astonishment. Ed is riveted.

ED

Wait a second. Don't move!

Ed excitedly jumps up, takes his napkin and covers the Doctor's face from the nose down.

ED

It's uncanny.

VAMPIRA

What's uncanny?

ED

Look at his skull!

CUT TO:

INT. BAPTIST CHURCH OF BEVERLY HILLS – DAY

Services are in progress. J. Edward Reynolds leads a CHOIR *singing an emotional spiritual.*

Ed, Tor, Criswell, Paul, Conrad, Vampira, Kathy, Bunny and Dr Tom Mason sit at the back. They're all wearing white robes and arguing about the Doctor.

TOR

He looks nutink like Bela!

CONRAD

He's kinda got his ears.

TOR

You're stupid!

KATHY

No, cover up his face.

Kathy lifts Dr Mason's robe over his bewildered face.

CRISWELL

Ah! Now I see it.

DR MASON
(*goofily imitating Bela*)
'I want to suck your blood!'

BUNNY

That's incredible
>   (*beat*)
Now call Karloff a cocksucker.

Everybody cracks up. Ed waves his arms.

ED

Shhh! We want these Baptists to like us.

Like bad kids, they quiet down. Ingenuous Southern REVEREND LYN
LEMON *speaks up front.*

REVEREND LEMON

Brothers and Sisters, we've reached a special part of the service.
The baptism of our new members!
>   (*beat*)
If the congregation will oblige, we'd like to adjourn and reconvene
at Emma DuBois's back yard.

EXT. BACK YARD — DAY

The straight-laced, devout CONGREGATION *is gathered around a large
swimming pool. Reverend Lemon, Reynolds and our misfits stand in the
shallow end, in their white robes.*

Criswell whispers to Vampira.

CRISWELL

Why couldn't we do this in the church?

VAMPIRA

Because 'Brother Tor' couldn't fit in the sacred tub.

Bunny nudges Ed.

BUNNY

How do you do it? How do you get all your friends to get *baptized*,
just so you can make a monster movie?

ED

It's not a monster movie. It's a supernatural thriller.

> BUNNY
> (*he nods*)

Point taken.

MONTAGE:

THE REVEREND BAPTIZES ED

> REVEREND LEMON
. . . Do you accept the Lord Jesus Christ as your Saviour?

> ED

I do.

Reynolds dunks Ed in the water.

THE REVEREND BAPTIZES BUNNY

> REVEREND LEMON
. . . Do you reject Satan and all his works?

> BUNNY
> (*hiding a smirk*)

Sure.

Reynolds dunks Buny.

*[THE REVEREND BAPTIZES TOR

> REVEREND LEMON
. . . Do you repent for all your sins?

> TOR

I do.

Tor winks slyly at Criswell.

Reynolds dunks Tor. But Tor slips from Reynolds' grasp and sinks to the bottom of the pool.

> REYNOLDS
Oh my God, I dropped him —

Tor lies on the bottom, staring lifelessly.

> CRISWELL

* Cut from completed film.

> (*mischievous*)
I don't think he's coming up!

REVEREND LEMON
Lord no! The man's drowning!

REYNOLDS
(*scared*)
What do we do?!

REVEREND LEMON
Help! *Help*!!!

The whole Congregation starts jumping in. Men and women in their Sunday finest leap into the pool and start tugging on Tor. But nobody can budge the big whale.

REVEREND LEMON
(*near tears*)
Dear Jesus, please forgive us!

ON TOR:

He suddenly rises, Poseidon-like, from the pool.

Tor spits out water, then lets out a hearty belly laugh.

TOR
Tor make good joke!

The Baptists aren't amused.]

CUT TO:

INT. CITY BUS — MORNING

A bus drives along. Every PASSENGER *stares at something up front — Vampira, in her slinky black outfit.* *[*She reads a* Graverobbers from Outer Space *script.*]

EXT. SCUMMY NEIGHBORHOOD — SAME TIME

The bus stops in a scary, run-down neighborhood. Vampira gets off and warily looks around.

* Cut from completed film.

153

This *can't* be the right address . . .

She nervously walks down a dingy alley, carrying an umbrella above her. Vampira gets to an unmarked grimy door, gulps, then slowly opens it . . .

INT. WAREHOUSE SOUNDSTAGE – DAY

And inside is the Graverobbers from Outer Space *famous cemetery set! The film is in production! Packed into a stinking little studio are a few scrawny twigs, branches and flimsy cardboard tombstones set against a black drop.*

****[**Tor struts about gregariously, in his 'Inspector Clay' suit. He chats up the* CREW.

TOR

I am so happy! Finally I am star with *dialogue*! I memorized every word. Eddie will be so proud!]

The Baptists chase Ed around. They wave the script.

REYNOLDS

Before we start shooting, Mr Wood, we have a few questions –

REVEREND LEMON

The script refers on numerous occasions to graverobbing. Now we find the concept of digging up consecrated ground highly offensive. It's blasphemy.

ED
(*very annoyed*)

What are you talking about?! It's the premise of the movie. It's even the title, for Christ's sake!

REVEREND LEMON
(*shocked*)

Mr Wood!

REYNOLDS

Yes, about that title, it strikes us as very inflammatory. Why don't we change it to *Plan 9 from Outer Space*?

---

* Cut from completed film.

Ed shakes his head.

ED

That's ridiculous!

WIPE TO:

INT. CEMETERY SET — DAY

They're filming the COPS *arriving at the pitch-black cemetery. There's a prop police car and an assistant blows fog in.*

ED

And, *action!*

Tor steps onto the set.

TOR
(as INSPECTOR CLAY)

'Medicul eksaminer been aroundt yet?'

COP

'Just left. The morgue wagon oughta be along most any time.'

TOR

'You get statement frumk witnesses?'

COP

'Yeah, but they're pretty scared.'

TOR

'Findink mess like dis oughta make anyone frightened. Have one of da boyz take dem back to town. You take jarge.'

ON THE CREW:

Everybody grimaces, trying to understand Tor. The SCRIPT GIRL *shakes her head.*

The Baptists angrily pull Ed aside.

REYNOLDS

What'd you give him all the lines for?? He's unintelligible!

ED

Look, Lugosi is dead and Vampira won't talk. I had to give *somebody* the dialogue.

REVEREND LEMON

That's not an answer.

WIPE TO:

INT. WAREHOUSE SOUNDSTAGE – LATER

Harry has painted half of Bunny's face green, like a Martian. The Baptists hover, watching.

*[MAKE-UP MAN HARRY

I'm telling ya, aliens are always green.

ED
(*irritated*)

No – it's an allegory! They should look like humans.

Ed aggressively wipes off Bunny's face.] Suddenly, Bunny tosses a handful of glitter onto his cheeks.

BUNNY

What about glitter? When I was a headliner in Paris, audiences loved it when I sparkled.

ED

No.

BUNNY

How about cat eyes?

ED

No!

BUNNY

Well, I certainly need an antenna.

ED

No!

* Cut from completed film.

156

> (*angry*)
> You're the ruler of the galaxy! Show a little *taste*!

INT. CEMETERY SET – LATER

As Inspector Clay, Tor wanders around the 'cemetery', waving his flashlight and nervously fingering his gun.

Ed grins at the Baptists.

> ED
> See, no talking. Isn't he good?
> > (*he grabs his megaphone*)
> *Cue Dr Tom!*

> DR TOM
> > (*off*)
> Now?

> ED
> *Yes, now! Lurk him. And be sure to keep your face covered!*

The door of a large papier-mâché crypt creeps open. Dr Tom uncertainly steps out, impersonating Bela. He holds the cape over his face and stalks Tor.

Ed is pleased as punch. He whispers to the Baptists.

> Isn't it wonderful? Bela lives!

> REVEREND LEMON
> Doesn't this strike you as a bit morbid?

> ED
> No, he would've loved it! Bela's returned from the grave – like Dracula.
> > (*he grabs the megaphone*)
> *Cue Vampira!*

Vampira steps out, walking in a trance. Tor is now cornered. He fruitlessly fires his gun, but bullets can't stop zombies. Vampira and Dr Tom kill him. Tor screams.

WIPE TO:

INT. CEMETERY SET – LATER

Paul and Conrad are scared cops exploring the cemetery.

> CONRAD (*as a* COP)
> 'Let's go down and find out whose grave it is.'

> PAUL MARCO (*as a* COP)
> 'Why do I always get hooked up with these spook details?
> Monsters! Graves! Bodies!'

> ED
> *Cue the flying saucer ray!*

Offstage, a grip on a ladder pans a 10K searchlight.

The light crosses the actors. They look up in horror, then clumsily fall down. A rickety fake tombstone tips over.

> ED
> And *perfect. Cut!*

> REYNOLDS
> (*freaking out*)
> 'Perfect'? Mr Wood, do you know *anything* about the art of film
> production?!

> ED
> I like to think so.

> REYNOLDS
> That cardboard headstone tipped over. This graveyard is obviously
> phony!

> ED
> People won't notice. Film-making isn't about the tiny details – it's
> about the big picture.

> REYNOLDS
> Oh, you wanna talk about the 'big picture'?! How 'bout that the
> policemen arrive in the daylight, but now it's suddenly night???

Ed suddenly flips out. He's livid.

ED

You don't know anything! Haven't you ever heard of 'suspension of disbelief'?!

A STRAPPING YOUNG MAN *walks up. He smiles at the Baptists.*

STRAPPING YOUNG MAN

Reverend, I'm here.

ED
(*baffled*)

Who's *he*?

REVEREND LEMON

This is our choir director. He's gonna play the young hero.

ED
(*furious*)

Are you *insane*?! *I'm* the director! *I* make the casting decisions around here!

REVEREND LEMON

I thought this was a group effort.

ED

Nooooo!!!

Ed spastically storms away.

INT. DRESSING ROOM – SAME TIME

Ed bursts in. He paces about, hysterically traumatized.

ED

They're driving me crazy! These Baptists are stupid, stupid, *stupid*!

Ed glances at a clothing rack – and sees an angora sweater.

Ed is taken aback. He slowly removes it from the hanger and rubs it against his face. His breathing slows.

ED

Mmm. I need to calm down . . . Take deep breaths . . .
(*he rubs the angora*)

159

Relax . . .

INT. SOUNDSTAGE – SAME TIME

The dressing-room door flies open. Ed slowly struts out, in the sweater, pantsuit and pumps. He is calmed and at ease.

The stage goes quiet. People are staring.

> ED
>
> Okay, everyone! Let's set up for Scene 112! Move the crypt stage left and get ready with Tor's make-up effect.

The crew resumes working. But the Baptists charge up, aghast.

> REVEREND LEMON
>
> Mr Wood? *What do you think you're doing?!*

> ED
>
> I'm directing.

> REYNOLDS
>
> Not like *that*, you're not!

> REVEREND LEMON
>
> Remove that get-up immediately. You shame our Lord.

Ed throws up his hands.

> ED
>
> That's it. I give up!

CUT TO:

EXT. SOUNDSTAGE – DAY

Ed frantically marches out of the building. He's still in his ladies' outfit. Ed sees a cab and whistles loudly.

The cab pulls over. Ed jumps in.

> ED
>
> Take me to the nearest bar.

CUT TO:

INT. MUSSO & FRANK'S – DAY

The place is quiet, mid-morning. Frazzled Ed enters and sits at the bar.

> ED
>
> Imperial whiskey, straight up.

The bartender nonchantly pours a shot. Ed takes the drink. He quietly sips his booze and reflects upon his day.

Ed glances around. And then, suddenly – his eyes widen.

Sitting at a table is ORSON WELLES! *The portly, world-famous film-maker sits alone, eating lunch with one hand and drawing storyboards with the other.*

Ed is thunderstruck.

> Oh my God. It's Orson Welles . . .

Ed nervously stands. He starts to step forward – when he catches his own reflection in a mirror. He's still in drag.

> Oh shit.

Ed rolls his eyes. He takes off his wig, then slowly approaches Orson Welles. Ed is terrified.

> Excuse me, sir . . .?

> ORSON WELLES
> (*he casually looks up*)
>
> Yes?

> ED
>
> Uh, uh, I'm a young film-maker, and a really big fan . . . and I just wanted to meet you.

> ORSON WELLES
> (*he extends his hand*)
>
> My pleasure. I'm Orson Welles.

> ED
>
> Oh. Um, I'm Ed Wood!
> (*he smiles anxiously*)
> So, what are you working on now?

ORSON WELLES

Eh, the financing just fell through for the third time on *Don Quixote*. *[So I'm trying to finish a promo for something else. But I can't find the soundtrack –
                    (*he shrugs*)
I think I left it in Malta.]

Ed is astonished.

ED

I can't believe it. These sound like *my* problems!

ORSON WELLES

It's the damn money men. You never know who's a windbag, and who's got the goods. And then they all think *they're* a director . . .

ED

Ain't that the truth! I've even had producers recut my movies –

ORSON WELLES

Ugh, I hate when that happens.

ED
                    (*on a roll*)
And they always want to cast their buddies – it doesn't even *matter* if they're right for the part!

ORSON WELLES

Tell me about it. I'm supposed to do a thriller at Universal, and they want Charlton Heston to play a *Mexican*!

Ed shakes his head. He's discouraged.

ED

Mr Welles, is it all worth it?

ORSON WELLES

It is when it works.
                    (*solemn*)
You know the one film of mine where I had total control? *Kane*. The studio hated it . . . but they didn't get to touch a frame.
                    (*he smiles warmly*)

* Cut from completed film.

162

Ed, visions are worth fighting for. Why spend your life making someone else's dreams?

CU – ED:

He has seen God.

> ED

Wow.

CUT TO:

INT. SOUNDSTAGE – DAY

Ed bursts onto the stage, a changed man. Re-energized, he confidently grabs the Baptists.

> ED

Mr Reynolds!

> REYNOLDS

Yes?

> ED

We are gonna finish this film *just the way I want it*! Because you can't compromise an artist's vision!

> REVEREND LEMON
> (*flustered*)

B-but it's our money –

> ED

And you're gonna make a bundle. This movie's gonna be famous! But only if you *shut up* and let me do it my way!

Reynolds and Reverend Lemon are speechless.

CU – ED:

He beams, turns and shouts triumphantly into the soundstage.

> ED
> *Alright! Actors in position! Let's finish this picture!!*

WIPE TO:

'PLAN 9' MONTAGE:

SCENE IN THE CEMETERY SET

Tor plays a zombie rising from the dead. He wears the scary white contact lenses. Tor's so big, he has trouble lifting himself from the grave.

*[EDITING ROOM

Ed and his stock-footage buddy watch a moviola.

ED

Okay, I want that tank! And I want that bomb!]

SCENE IN THE SPACESHIP SET

Bunny's make-up is back to normal. He wears an alien commander suit. A HAMMY ALIEN enters and salutes with a bizarre arm-crossing gesture.

[Ed leans into the foreground. He whispers to Harry.

ED

Now *that's* an alien.

Behind Ed, the scene plays.]

BUNNY

'What plan will we follow?'

HAMMY ALIEN

'Plan 9.'

BUNNY

'Plan 9 . . .'
(*he consults his papers*)
'Ah yes. Plan 9 deals with the resurrection of the dead.'

*[SCENE IN THE CEMETERY SET

Zombie Tor staggers up to Paul Marco and clobbers him.]

OFFSTAGE

Ed smiles at the Baptists.

ED

Maybe you guys were right. *Plan 9 is* a good title.

* Cut from completed film.

164

MINIATURE CITY SET

Ed shoots the famous flying saucers. Paul holds a paper plate and Conrad lights it on fire.

The 'saucer' soars on fishing line over a little miniature town.

*[SCENE IN THE BEDROOM SET

Dr Tom glides in, his cape over his face. A woman screams.]

COCKPIT SET

Ed stands in front of a masonite board and two chairs. An actor playing the AIRPLANE PILOT *walks up.*

PILOT

Where's the cockpit set?

ED

You're standing in it.
(*he yells off*)
Alright, bring in the shower curtain!

A shower curtain gets lowered into the doorway.

*[EXT. DUSTY ROAD

A car zooms by. Kathy drives, as Ed shoots handheld out the back window.]

SCENE IN THE SPACESHIP SET

The Hammy Alien argues with the humans.

PILOT

'So what if we develop this solarnite bomb? We'd be even a stronger nation.'

HAMMY ALIEN

'Stronger? You see! You see!! Your stupid minds! Stupid! *Stupid!*'

PILOT

'That's all I'm taking from you.'

---

* Cut from completed film.

He whacks the alien. A brawl breaks out.

SCENE WITH CRISWELL

Criswell lectures behind a desk, with mysterious lighting.

> CRISWELL
>
> Greetings my friends. We are all interested in the future, for that is where we will spend the rest of our lives.

SCENE IN THE CEMETERY SET

The famous shot: Tor and Vampira walk in a trance through the foggy cemetery.

Offstage, Ed stands with the crew. He shouts gleefully.

> ED
> *(he beams)*
>
> And *cut! Print it! It's a wrap!*

END MONTAGE

CUT TO:

*[EXT. CITY – NIGHT

It's pouring rain. Standing in the drench is Ed. He's wearing a tux and fighting with his open convertible top. The Nash Rambler is filled with water.

> ED
>
> I can't get it to go up.

Kathy stands under an awning. She wears a pretty gown.

> KATHY
>
> Ed, you're gonna miss your own première.

> ED
> *(he gives up)*
>
> C'mon! Let's just go.

Ed impulsively opens the car door. Water pours out. Kathy scurries out and jumps in the wet car with him.]

* Cut from completed film.

EXT. PANTAGES MOVIE THEATER – NIGHT

The rain is gushing down. The marquee proclaims 'WORLD PREMIÈRE: "PLAN 9 FROM OUTER SPACE!"'

People hurry in. Ed and Kathy roar up in the open convertible. It begins to rain. Unable to raise the top, Ed leaves it open and runs into the theater with Kathy.

INT. PANTAGES THEATER – NIGHT

The theater is packed. All the gang, and their friends and families, are gathered.

Criswell stands onstage, speaking into a mike.

> CRISWELL
> You are about to see an extraordinary motion picture. But before it begins, I think we ought to give a hand to the man without whom we wouldn't be here tonight . . . Eddie, take a bow!

The crowd erupts in applause. Everybody goes crazy – even the Baptists. People yell 'Speech! Speech!'

Ed smiles proudly. Kathy kisses him. Ed runs down front, hugs Criswell, then takes the microphone.

> ED
> Thanks a million. I just wanna say . . . this film is for Bela.

The lights dim.

DISSOLVE TO:

INT. THEATER – MINUTES LATER

The title 'PLAN 9 FROM OUTER SPACE' is projected onto the screen. As random images from the film play out, we drift over the happy faces of our friends watching.

Paul and Conrad stare, enthralled.

Tor laughs as he sees himself.

Vampira giggles. Bunny nudges her playfully.

167

Criswell mouths his own lines.

ONSCREEN:

Bela appears in his little suit. In the last footage he ever shot, he shuffles around in front of his house, then tenderly smells the flower.

ON ED:

He watches, entranced. Then he smiles to himself.

> ED
> This is the one. This is the one I'll be remembered for.

CUT TO:

*[INT. THEATER LOBBY – LATER

The boisterous crowd is in high spirits. People congratulate Ed and pat him on the back. 'It was great!' 'It's your best one yet!' 'Bela would've loved it!'

Ed drifts through the crowd, basking in the glory. It's like a wonderful dream.]

EXT. THEATER – SAME TIME

The rain comes down in sheets. The doors burst open, and Ed and Kathy run out.

> KATHY
> Ed, I'm so happy for you.

> ED
> Let's get married.

> KATHY
> *(starled)*
> Huh?!

> ED
> *Right now.* Let's drive to Vegas!

---

* Cut from completed film.

KATHY

But it's pouring. And the car top is stuck!

ED
(he gives his killer grin)

So? It's only a five-hour drive. And it'll probably clear up, once we hit the desert. Heck, it'll probably clear up once we drive around the corner. I promise.

Kathy stares in disbelief. Then she smiles. They kiss.

Ed and Kathy jump into the open convertible. Water pours out. The engine starts and they drive away, disappearing into the pouring rain.

A moment.

And then, we move up, up, into the black clouds. Lightning cracks across the sky.

*[OPTICAL:

We slowly pull out from the sky, move through a window . . . and we're back inside:

INT. HAUNTED MANSION PARLOR – NIGHT

Criswell is sitting inside his coffin. He stares at us.

CRISWELL

My friend, you have just seen the story of Edward D. Wood, Junior. Stranger than fact . . . and yet every incident based on sworn testimony.
(his eyes gleam)
A man. A life. Can you prove it didn't happen?

A beat, to ponder this. And then Criswell slowly lies back in his coffin, and the lid mysteriously closes over him.]

FADE OUT

EPILOGUE: CLOSING BIOGRAPHIES

EDWARD D. WOOD, JR *kept struggling in Hollywood, but mainstream success eluded him. After a slow descent into alcoholism and monster*

* Cut from completed film.

nudie films, he died in 1978, at the age of fifty-four.

Two years later, Ed was voted 'Worst Director of All Time', bringing him worldwide acclaim and a new generation of fans.

KATHY WOOD *was married to Ed for over twenty years, loyal throughout many ups and downs. After his death, she never remarried.*

BELA LUGOSI *never rose from the grave, but after appearing in 103 films, he is more famous than ever. Today, his movie memorabilia outsells Boris Karloff's by a substantial margin.*

BUNNY BRECKINRIDGE, *despite much talk, never actually had his sex change. He is currently living in New Jersey.*

DOLORES FULLER *after leaving Ed, went on to a successful songwriting career. Her compositions include the Elvis Presley hits 'Rock-a-Hula Baby' and 'Do the Clam'.*

TOR JOHNSON *appear in numerous 'B' movies, before achieving his greatest fame as a best-selling Hallowe'en mask. He died in 1971.*

VAMPIRA *retired from showbusiness to sell handcrafted jewelry. In the 1980s, she unsuccessfully sued Elvira for stealing her act.*

DR TOM MASON *appeared in one more Ed Wood film,* Night of the Ghouls. *This time, Ed let the late chiropractor show his face.*

PAUL MARCO *and* CONRAD BROOKS *are still personalities on the Hollywood scene. Paul is founder and president of the Paul Marco Fan Club. The* New York Times *recently named Conrad the 'Gielgud of Bad Movies'.*

CRISWELL *continued making highly inaccurate and bizarre predictions, often as a guest on* The Tonight Show. *He departed our dimension in 1982.*

THE END